Computation in Science
(Second Edition)

From concepts to practice

Computation in Science
(Second Edition)

From concepts to practice

Konrad Hinsen

Centre de Biophysique Moléculaire, CNRS Orléans, Orléans, France

IOP Publishing, Bristol, UK

ISBN   978-0-7503-3287-3 (ebook)
ISBN   978-0-7503-3285-9 (print)
ISBN   978-0-7503-3288-0 (myPrint)
ISBN   978-0-7503-3286-6 (mobi)

DOI   10.1088/978-0-7503-3287-3

Version: 20200901

IOP ebooks

British Library Cataloguing-in-Publication Data: A catalogue record for this book is available from the British Library.

Published by IOP Publishing, wholly owned by The Institute of Physics, London

IOP Publishing, Temple Circus, Temple Way, Bristol, BS1 6HG, UK

US Office: IOP Publishing, Inc., 190 North Independence Mall West, Suite 601, Philadelphia, PA 19106, USA

Contents

Preface

In the course of only a few decades, computers have revolutionized scientific research and have become indispensable tools for both experimentalists and theoreticians. More and more scientists are writing computer programs for doing their work, and practically all scientists today use computer programs written by somebody else. Sometimes they do so without even being aware of it, in particular when these programs are integrated into lab instruments.

In spite of the ubiquitous use of computers in science, few researchers in the natural sciences have any formal training in computer science, software engineering, or numerical analysis. They usually acquire their computing knowledge 'on the job', and as a consequence it is usually limited to the practical knowledge required for applying computational tools. A big part of this practical knowledge is about specific computing technologies which, given the fast pace of change in this field, tend to be short-lived. Scientists often feel overwhelmed by the amount of computing knowledge they have to absorb, while at the same time lacking a solid understanding of the basic principles of the field.

The goal of this book is to explain these basic principles, and to show how they relate to the tasks of a scientist's daily work in the research lab. It provides a high-level overview of those aspects of computer science and software engineering that are most relevant for computational science, using a language familiar to scientists, and places them into the context of scientific computing. References to the literature are provided for readers wishing to study a particular aspect in more depth. My hope is that this book will allow its readers to use computers with more confidence, and to see computing technologies in a different light, evaluating them on the basis of how they contribute to doing better science.

The intended audience for this book includes both graduate students and experienced scientists. Some hands-on experience with computing is highly desirable, but no competence in any particular computing technology is expected. Most of this book is relevant to all of the natural sciences. The frontier between the physical and the life sciences is blurring, and computation plays a big part in this change. An interdisciplinary approach to computational science therefore seems the most appropriate one for the 21st century. Its main drawback is that some misunderstandings are inevitable. Even a term as basic as 'theory' or 'model' can have different meanings in different fields. My own background in theoretical physics will certainly show through occasionally. If anything I say seems strange or wrong, please consider that this may just reflect a cultural difference.

The website at http://computation-in-science.khinsen.net/ contains complementary material to this book, in particular references to on-line material that I consider of interest for my readers. I will regularly add new references that I discover and remove links that no longer work.

Acknowledgements

In writing this book, critical comments from a diverse team of reviewers have been invaluable. My thanks go to Jane Charlesworth, Alice della Penna, Javier Galgarra, Jeremy Gray, Chris Ing, Arnaud Legrand, Tim Rice, and in particular Ian Hawke. They have all provided valuable feedback to drafts of the text, which I hope to have used wisely for improving the presentation.

Author biography

Konrad Hinsen

Konrad Hinsen is a research scientist with a background in statistical physics. He develops and uses computational methods for the study of complex systems. Most of his work centers around the structure and dynamics of proteins, at the interface of theory and experiment. He holds a PhD in physics from RWTH Aachen University, and conducts his research at the Centre de Biophysique Moléculaire in Orléans and at the Synchrotron SOLEIL in Saint Aubin. In addition to his research activity, he teaches courses on computational science and works as a department editor for *Computing in Science and Engineering* magazine.

IOP Publishing

Computation in Science (Second Edition)
From concepts to practice
Konrad Hinsen

Chapter 1

What is computation?

This book is about computation in the context of scientific research. Scientists should always try to be precise about what they say, so I will start by explaining what this term actually means. It turns out that this is not as trivial as it may seem to be. Moreover, there are also pragmatic reasons for discussing the nature of computation, because a good grasp of what computation actually *is* makes it much easier to appreciate what it can and cannot be used for in scientific research.

Common dictionary definitions of computation are remarkably imprecise. Oxford proposes 'the action of mathematical calculation' or 'the use of computers, especially as a subject of research or study'. Merriam-Webster has 'the act or action of computing: calculation' or 'the use or operation of a computer' but also 'a system of reckoning'. Both dictionaries refer to 'calculation', but do not provide useful definitions for that word either. The vagueness of these dictionary definitions can be traced back to the long-lasting confusion about what computation is and how it relates to mathematics. It was only the development of formal logic and mathematical formalism in the early 20th century that led to a precise definition of computation, which helped to pave the way to the development of automatic computing machines. This definition is the topic of section 1.1.

Beyond the exploration of what defines computation, I will also look at what computation is for scientists, i.e. *why* computation is so important in scientific research. Most scientists probably think of computers and computation as tools that they use to process experimental data or mathematical equations. However, there are other roles that computation plays in science, and which I will briefly discuss in section 1.2.

1.1 Defining computation

1.1.1 Numerical computation

The most familiar computations are the numerical calculations that we all do in everyday life: adding up prices, multiplying the length and width of a room to

doi:10.1088/978-0-7503-3287-3ch1

compute its surface, dividing a quantity into equal parts, etc. Most people today have even more occasions for doing numerical calculations in their professional lives. Basic arithmetic on anything that can be quantified is so fundamental that it takes up a significant part of training in the first years of school. Mechanical aids for numerical operations, such as the abacus, have been used for at least 2000 years and perhaps even for much longer.

We do not think much about how we do simple arithmetic operations on small numbers, and in fact we often just recall the result that we have internalized due to frequent use. But as soon as we work on larger numbers, mental calculation becomes a mechanical activity based on rules we have learned. An example for such a rule is: to multiply a number by 9, multiply it by ten and then subtract the original number.

When operations become too complex to be handled in the head, we turn to pen and paper for a more reliable record of the intermediate results in our calculations. A large number of calculation techniques with pen and paper have been developed in the course of the centuries, ranging from addition via long division to the calculation of cube roots.

As a simple example, consider adding the numbers 173 and 51. One way to do it systematically starts by writing one below the other, adding zeros to the left of the smaller number to make the number of digits equal:

$$1\ 7\ 3$$
$$0\ 5\ 1$$

We then process the digits from right to left, starting by adding 3 and 1. We 'know' that the result is 4, because we have done this so often. But for the slightly more complex operation of multiplication, most readers probably remember how they memorized multiplication tables in school—tables that were actually printed in books. To be precise in our description of addition, we will use an equally explicit addition table for one-digit integers:

	0	1	2	3	4	5	6	7	8	9
0	0	1	2	3	4	5	6	7	8	9
1	1	2	3	4	5	6	7	8	9	0
2	2	3	4	5	6	7	8	9	0	1
3	3	4	5	6	7	8	9	0	1	2
4	4	5	6	7	8	9	0	1	2	3
5	5	6	7	8	9	0	1	2	3	4
6	6	7	8	9	0	1	2	3	4	5
7	7	8	9	0	1	2	3	4	5	6
8	8	9	0	1	2	3	4	5	6	7
9	9	0	1	2	3	4	5	6	7	8

We actually need *two* such tables, the second one being for the 'carry' digit, which is 1 when the sum of the two digits is 10 or more, and which is 0 otherwise. We note the one-digit sum and the carry digit, and move on to the left to handle the next digit:

$$
\begin{array}{r}
1\ 7\ 3 \\
0\ 5\ 1 \\
0 \\
\hline
4
\end{array}
\quad \rightarrow \quad
\begin{array}{r}
1\ 7\ 3 \\
0\ 5\ 1 \\
1 \\
\hline
2\ 4
\end{array}
\quad \rightarrow \quad
\begin{array}{r}
1\ 7\ 3 \\
0\ 5\ 1 \\
\hline
2\ 2\ 4
\end{array}
$$

This method, and all the other arithmetic operations we use, rely on the positional notation for numbers that is used all around the world today. Any natural number can be written as a sequence of the digits 0 to 9. Another symbol, the minus sign, takes care of negative integers, an one further symbol, either the decimal point or the division slash, makes it possible to express fractions. The rules for arithmetic can then be formulated as rules for manipulating sequences of symbols, as shown above for addition, which can be applied mechanically.

1.1.2 From numbers to symbols

It is indeed important to realize that the method outlined above does not work on *numbers*, but on a specific *representation* for numbers. Numbers are an abstract concept, which cannot be manipulated using mechanical rules. Different representations lead to different methods for doing arithmetic. Even though the decimal character string '42', the roman-numeral character string 'XLII', and the English-language character string 'forty-two' refer to the same number, they cannot be manipulated in the same way. In fact, our recipe for addition never refers to numbers. It takes two sequences of digits as input, and produces one sequence of digits as output. Applying the recipe does not require any knowledge of numbers, only the capacity to work with a finite set of symbols and apply rules to them.

A recipe for solving a specific problem by manipulating symbols is called an *algorithm*. The word is derived from the name of the Persian mathematician al-Khwārizmī who lived in the 9th century. His book describing the 'Indian numbers', which today we call Arabic numerals, introduced our modern decimal notation and its rules for arithmetic into Europe [1]. The use of this system was called 'algorism' in the late middle ages, and later the spelling and meaning transformed into today's 'algorithm'. The positional notation for numbers transformed arithmetic from a difficult craft performed by trained specialists into a routine task that could be mastered by almost everyone.

Today the decimal representation of numbers seems so obvious to us that we often make no difference between a number and its decimal representation. This phenomenon is not limited to numbers. We rarely distinguish carefully between a word and its meaning either, and in quantum physics, to cite an example from science, the confusion between a quantum state and one of its many possible representations is very common. When thinking about computation, it is often important to recall that the Universe of symbols and the Universe of meanings are separate. In computer science, this is known as the distinction between *syntax* and *semantics*. Syntax defines which sequences of symbols a particular algorithm deals with, for example 'a sequence of any number of the digits 0 to 9'. Semantics defines how such sequences of symbols are interpreted, such as 'a natural number'. No knowledge of semantics is needed to *apply* our algorithm for adding two natural numbers, but it is essential to understand what the algorithm does, and in particular which problems it can help to solve.

A symptom of the confusion between numbers and their representations is the popular saying that 'computers work only on numbers'. This is patently false: what today's digital computers work on is sequences of bits, a bit being a symbol from an alphabet containing two symbols. We often choose the digits 0 and 1 to represent this alphabet, suggesting an interpretation as binary numbers, i.e. numbers represented in a positional notation with base 2. The idea that computers work on numbers is mistaken because bits can equally well represent information other than numbers. It is also misleading in another way because it suggests that any number-related problem can be solved by a computer. However, most numbers cannot be represented by sequences of bits and therefore cannot enter in any computation.

It is easy to see that bits can represent any information at all that can be written as sequences of symbols. Suppose we have an alphabet with N symbols, for example the $N = 26$ letters of the English alphabet. We can then make up a translation table that assigns a unique set of values for five bits to each symbol in our alphabet. With five bits, we have $2^5 = 32$ distinct values, so six values will be left unused. Our translation table allows us to encode any English word in terms of bit sequences.

It is less obvious and perhaps even surprising to many readers that most numbers cannot be represented as bit sequences. For natural numbers, there is no problem: any sequence of bits can be interpreted as a natural number in base 2 notation. Inversely, every natural number can be written in base 2 notation, and therefore as a sequence of bits. It is thus possible to define a one-to-one correspondence between natural numbers and bit sequences. In mathematical terminology, the set of natural numbers is isomorphic to the set of bit sequences. Since we can perform computations on sequences of bits, we can perform computations on natural numbers. In fact, any set of values that we wish to do computations on must be isomorphic to the set of bit sequences, or equivalently to the set of natural numbers, or to a subset of such a set. Such sets are called *countable*. All finite sets are countable: just write down the elements in some order and then write a number below to each element, starting from 1. Infinite sets that are countable are called *countably infinite* sets.

It is straightforward to see that integers are still countable: use one bit for the sign, and then a natural-number bit sequence for the absolute value. It takes a bit more effort to show that the rational numbers, i.e. the set of all quotients of integers, are countable. By the definition of countability, this requires the assignment of a unique natural number to each rational number. The standard procedure is based on a two-dimensional matrix-like arrangement of the rational numbers:

$$\frac{1}{1} \; \frac{2}{1} \; \frac{3}{1} \; \frac{4}{1} \cdots$$

$$\frac{1}{2} \; \frac{2}{2} \; \frac{3}{2} \; \frac{4}{2} \cdots$$

$$\frac{1}{3} \; \frac{2}{3} \; \frac{3}{3} \; \frac{4}{3} \cdots$$

$$\frac{1}{4} \; \frac{2}{4} \; \frac{3}{4} \; \frac{4}{4} \cdots$$

$$\vdots \; \vdots \; \vdots \; \vdots \; \ddots$$

The entries of this infinite matrix can now be enumerated along diagonals:

$$
\begin{array}{lllll}
1 & 3 & 6 & 10 & 15 \cdots \\
2 & 5 & 9 & 14 & \cdots \\
4 & 8 & 13 & & \cdots \\
7 & 12 & & & \cdots \\
11 & & & & \cdots \\
\vdots & \vdots & \vdots & \vdots & \vdots & \ddots
\end{array}
$$

A more sophisticated enumeration scheme would skip over each number that is equal to one that already received an index earlier. For example, 2/2 would be skipped because it is equal to 1/1.

The proof that the set of real numbers is *not* countable is more involved, and I will not reproduce it here. Like many other proofs concerning infinite sets, it goes back to Georg Cantor, a German mathematician who laid the foundations of set theory in the late 19th century, and actually provided the first rigorous definition of the real numbers. The complex numbers, being a superset of the real numbers, are also uncountable. There are, however, countable number sets larger than the rational numbers. A well-known one in mathematics is the set of *algebraic numbers*, defined as the roots of polynomials with integer coefficients. In the context of computation, the largest useful countable subset of the real numbers is the set of *computable numbers*, which was introduced by Alan Turing in the same 1936 publication as the Turing machine. I will come back to this subject in chapters 2 and 3, because it is of central importance for the use of computation in science.

We can now write down a first definition of computation, which will be refined in chapter 3:

Computation is the transformation of sequences of symbols according to precise rules.

What will need refinement is the 'precise rules', which must be expressed so precisely that a machine can apply them unambiguously.

1.1.3 Non-numerical computation

Once we get rid of the idea that computation is about numbers, we can easily identify other operations that qualify as computations. One example is solving equations by algebraic manipulations. The steps leading from

$$y + 2x = z$$

to

$$x = \frac{1}{2}\left(z - y\right)$$

are completely mechanical and can be formulated as an algorithm. The practical evidence is that computers can do the job. Software packages that implement such operations are called *computer algebra* systems, emphasizing algebraic manipulations. However, computer algebra systems also perform other non-numerical algorithms, for example finding the derivative or integral of an elementary function. The algorithm for computing derivatives is simple and taught in every calculus course. In contrast, the algorithm for computing indefinite integrals is very complicated [2] and was first implemented as a computer program only in 1987 [3].

A perhaps more surprising use of computation in mathematics is the validation of proofs. A proof is a sequence of deduction steps, each of which establishes the truth of a statement based on other statements already known to be true and a finite set of rules of logic deduction. In textbooks and mathematical publications, proofs are written concisely for human readers who have a prior knowledge of mathematics. But when all the details are spelled out, proofs consist of nothing but applications of a finite set of deduction rules. These rules are applied to statements that must respect the rules of a formal language. The use of computers to check such detailed proofs is becoming more and more common, both in mathematical research and in industrial applications. This involves writing the proof in some formal language, as a sequence of symbols. The 'proof checking' computation transforms this sequence of symbols into a 'true' or 'false' statement about the proof's validity.

Leaving the narrow scope of mathematics, we find a huge number of domains where computation is applied to textual data. Finding a word in a text is a computation: it transforms the input data (the text and the word to look for) into output data (the position in the text where the word occurs), both of which can be encoded as sequences of symbols. Likewise, aligning two DNA sequences, translating a sentence from English to French, or compiling a Fortran program, are computations in which the data being processed are text. In fact, numbers and text are the two kinds of elementary data from which almost everything else is made up by composition: images are represented as two-dimensional arrays of numbers, dictionaries as sets of word pairs, etc. However, this fundamental role of numbers and text is due to their importance to humans, not computers.

Another kind of data that are becoming increasingly important for scientific computation are graphs, in particular when used to describe networks. Traffic flow, protein interactions in a cell, and molecular structures are all examples of what can be described by graphs. An example of a computation on graphs is a check for cycles. This transforms the input data (a graph) into output data (a list of all cycles in the graph). Encoding graphs, cycles, and lists as sequences of symbols is not as obvious as encoding numbers and text. Humans already represented numbers and text by sequences of symbols long before thinking about computers and computation. The human representation of graphs, on the other hand, takes the form of two-dimensional drawings. The precise techniques for representing graphs as sequences of symbols are beyond the scope of this book, but I will come back to the general question of information representation in computers in section 5.3.2.

1.2 The roles of computation in scientific research

Computation as a tool

The most visible role of computation in scientific research is its use as a tool. Experimentalists process their raw data, for example to correct for artifacts of their equipment. Then they fit a theoretical model to their data by adjusting parameters. Theoreticians compute numerical predictions from a model, in order to compare them to experimental results. Both experimentalists and theoreticians make heavy use of computation for understanding their data, in particular using visualization techniques.

It is worth making a distinction between *computation* as a tool and *computers* as a tool. Computers perform computations, but they also deal with other tasks. Scientists use computers for communicating with their peers, looking up information in Wikipedia, and for controlling lab equipment. None of these tasks involve much visible computation, though there is computation going on under the hood. Today's computers are as much communication devices as computation devices.

Computation for understanding

Richard Feynman had written on his blackboard: 'What I cannot create, I do not understand.' We cannot understand a theory, a model, or an approximation, unless we have done something with it. One way to gain experience with mathematical models is to apply them to concrete situations. Another one, even more powerful, is to implement them as computer programs. Donald Knuth has expressed this very succinctly [4]:

> It has often been said that a person does not really understand something until he teaches it to someone else. Actually a person does not really understand something until he can teach it to a computer, i.e. express it as an algorithm. The attempt to formalize things as algorithms leads to a much deeper understanding than if we simply try to comprehend things in the traditional way.

The utility of writing programs for understanding scientific concepts and mathematical models comes from the extreme rigor and precision required in programming. Communication between humans relies on shared knowledge, starting with the definition of the words of everyday language. A typical scientific article assumes the reader to have significant specialist knowledge in science and mathematics. Even a mathematical proof, probably the most precise kind of statement in the scientific literature, assumes many definitions and theorems to be known by the reader, without even providing a list of them. A computer has no such prior knowledge. We must communicate with a computer in a formal language which is precisely defined, i.e. there are clear rules, verifiable by a computer, that define what is and what isn't a valid expression in the language. Every aspect of our science that somehow impacts a computed result must be expressed in this formal language in order to obtain a working computer program.

Another reason why writing a program is often useful for understanding a mathematical model is that an algorithm is necessarily constructive. In the physical sciences, most theories take the form of differential equations. These equations fully *define* their solutions, and are also useful for reasoning about their general properties, but provide no obvious way of *finding* one. Writing a computer program requires, first of all, to think about what this program *does*, and then about *how* it should go about this.

Implementing a scientific model as a computer program also has the advantage that, as a bonus, you get a tool for exploring the consequences of the model for simple applications. Computer-aided exploration is another good way to gain a better understanding of a scientific model (see [5, 6] for some outstanding examples). In the study of complex systems, with models that are directly formulated as algorithms, computational exploration is often the only approach to gaining scientific insight [7].

Computation as a form of scientific knowledge

A computer program that implements a theoretical model, for example a program written with the goal of understanding this model, is a peculiar written representation of this model. It is therefore an expression of scientific knowledge, much like a textbook or a journal article. We will see in the following chapters that much scientific knowledge can be expressed in the form of computer programs, and that much of today's scientific knowledge exists in fact *only* in the form of computer programs, because the traditional scientific knowledge representations cannot handle complex structured information. This raises important questions for the future of computational science, which I will return to in chapter 7.

Computation as a model for information processing in nature

Computers are physical devices that are designed by engineers to perform computation. Many other engineered devices perform computation as well, though usually with much more limited capacity. The classic example from computer science textbooks is a vending machine, which translates operator input (pushing buttons, inserting coins) into actions (deliver goods), a task that requires computation. Of course a vending machine does more than compute, and as users we are most interested in that additional behavior. Nevertheless, information processing, and thus computation, is an important aspect of the machine's operation.

The same is true of many systems that occur in nature. A well-known example is the process of cell division, common to all biological organisms, which involves copying and processing information stored in the form of DNA [8]. Another example of a biological process that relies on information processing is plant growth [9]. Most animals have a nervous system, a part of the body that is almost entirely dedicated to information processing. Neuroscience, which studies the nervous system, has close ties to both biology and computer science. This is also true of cognitive science, which deals with processes of the human mind that are increasingly modeled using computation.

Of course, living organisms are not *just* computers. Information processing in organisms is inextricably combined with other processes. In fact, the identification of computation as an isolated phenomenon, and its realization by engineered devices that perform a precise computation any number of times, with as little dependence on their environment as is technically possible, is a hallmark of human engineering that has no counterpart in nature. Nevertheless, focusing on the computational aspects of life, and writing computer programs to simulate information processing in living organisms, has significantly contributed to a better understanding of their function.

On a much grander scale, one can consider all physical laws as rules for information processing, and conclude that the whole Universe is a giant computer. This idea was first proposed in 1967 by German computer pioneer Konrad Zuse [10] and has given rise to a field of research called *digital physics*, situated at the intersection of physics, philosophy, and computer science [11].

1.3 Analog computing

What I have discussed above, and what I will discuss in the rest of this book, is computation in the tradition of arithmetic and Boolean logic, automated by digital computers. There is, however, a very different approach to tackling some of the same problems, which is known as *analog computing*. Its basic idea is to construct systems whose behavior is governed by the mathematical relations one wishes to explore, and then perform experiments on these systems. The simplest analog computer is the *slide rule*, which was a common tool to perform multiplication and division (plus a few more complex operations) before the general availability of electronic calculators.

Today, analog computers have almost disappeared from scientific research, because digital computers perform most tasks better and at a much lower cost. This is also the reason why this book's focus is on digital computing. However, analog computing is still used for some specialized applications. More importantly, the idea of computation as a form of experiment has persisted in the scientific community. Whereas I consider it inappropriate in the context of software-controlled digital computers, as I will explain in section 5.1, it is a useful point of view to adopt in looking at emerging alternative computing techniques, such as artificial neural networks.

1.4 Further reading

Computation has its roots in numbers and arithmetic, a story that is told by Georges Ifrah in *The universal History of Numbers* [12].

Video courses explaining basic arithmetic are provided by the Khan Academy. It is instructive to follow them with an eye on the algorithmic symbol-processing aspect of each technique.

The use of computation for understanding has been emphasized in the context of physics by Sussman and Wisdom [13]. They developed an original approach to teaching classical mechanics by means of computation [14], which is available online, as is complementary material from a corresponding MIT course. The authors used the same approach in a course on differential geometry [15], available online as well.

The Bootstrap project uses games programming for teaching mathematical concepts to students in the 12–16 year age range. An example of computing as a teaching aid in university-level mathematics has been described by Ionescu and Jansson [16].

Computer programming is also starting to be integrated into science curricula because of its utility for understanding. See the textbook by Langtangen [17] for an example.

A very accessible introduction to the ideas of digital physics is given by Stephen Wolfram in his essay 'What is ultimately possible in physics?' [18].

References

[1] Crossley J N and Henry A S 1990 Thus spake al-Khwārizmī: A translation of the text of Cambridge University Library Ms. Ii.vi.5 *Hist. Math.* **17** 103–31

[2] Risch R H 1969 The problem of integration in finite terms Trans *Am. Math. Soc* **139** 167–88

[3] Bronstein M 1990 Integration of elementary functions *J. Symb. Comput.* **9** 117–73

[4] Knuth D E 1974 Computer science and its relation to mathematics *Am. Math. Mon.* **81** 323–43

[5] Victor B Kill Math http://worrydream.com/KillMath/.

[6] Victor B Media for Thinking the Unthinkable http://worrydream.com/#!/MediaForThinking TheUnthinkable.

[7] Downey A B 2012 *Think Complexity: Complexity Science and Computational Modeling* 1st edn (Sebastopol, CA: O'Reilly)

[8] Xing J, Mather W and Hong C 2014 Computational cell biology: past, present and future *Interface Focus* **4** 20140027

[9] Prusinkiewicz P, Hanan J S, Fracchia F D, Lindenmayer A, Fowler D R, de Boer M J M and Mercer L 1996 The Algorithmic Beauty of Plants *The Virtual Laboratory* (New York: Springer)

[10] Zuse K 1970 *Calculating Space* (Boston, MA: MIT Press) Technical Translation AZT-70-164-GEMIT https://www.worldscientific.com/doi/abs/10.1142/9789814374309_0036

[11] Zenil H (ed) 2013 *A Computable Universe: Understanding and Exploring Nature as Computation* (Singapore: World Scientific)

[12] Ifrah G 2000 *The Universal History of Numbers: From Prehistory to the Invention of the Computer* vol 1 (New York: Wiley)

[13] Sussman G J and Wisdom J 2002 The role of programming in the formulation of ideas *Technical Report AIM-2002-018* MIT Artificial Intelligence Laboratory http://hdl.handle.net/1721.1/6707

[14] Sussman G and Wisdom J 2001 *Structure and Interpretation of Classical Mechanics* (Cambridge, MA: MIT Press)

[15] Sussman G J, Wisdom J and Farr W 2013 *Functional Differential Geometry* (Cambridge, MA: The MIT Press)

[16] Ionescu C and Jansson P 2016 Domain-specific languages of mathematics: presenting mathematical analysis using functional programming *Electron. Proc. Theor. Comput. Sci.* **230** pp 1–15

[17] Langtangen H P 2016 A Primer on Scientific Programming with Python *Texts in Computational Science and Engineering* vol 6 (Berlin: Springer)

[18] Wolfram S 2012 What Is ultimately possible in physics? *A Computable Universe* ed H Zenil (Singapore: World Scientific) pp 417–33 https://www.stephenwolfram.com/publications/what-ultimately-possible-physics/

Chapter 2

Computation in science

Computation has always been an important tool for scientists, whose work is centered around measurements and quantitative theoretical models. Numerical computations are indispensable for obtaining numbers from mathematical equations. In fact, the development of various computing machines since the 17th century was to a large degree motivated by the computational needs of physics and astronomy. Non-numerical computations, in particular in algebra and calculus, have been an important part of doing science for several centuries as well, and the use of electronic computers for such tasks goes back to the 1960s, when the first machines became available to research laboratories.

In addition to being tools that facilitate the previously laborious task of processing and analyzing experimental data and theoretical models, computers are introducing profound changes in the nature of scientific models. Large-scale simulations and complex statistical approaches to analyzing large datasets do not fit neatly into the traditional 'two pillar' view of science as an interplay between theory and experiment. The main part of this chapter looks at the many ways in which computation is used in science today, and how they relate to its traditional pillars, experiment and theory. It is an invitation for the reader to reflect about his or her own use of computational methods. Which models are they based on? Which approximations are involved? How can those approximations be tested or justified? What can go wrong in applying the methods, and how can the risk of mistakes be kept to a minimum? These are, of course, the same questions that theoreticians have always asked about scientific models and methods. But this task has become much more difficult in the digital age because theoretical models are now separated from their users by an often opaque layer made of software. There is an increasing tendency to use computational methods as black-box tools, judged according to pragmatic criteria such as convenience or performance, often disregarding its scientific qualities such as correctness or appropriateness for a situation, which are more difficult to assess. I would like to encourage computational scientists to open these black boxes and understand what is going on inside.

The example that I have chosen for illustrating the different types of scientific models and how they relate to computation is the study of the motion of celestial bodies, which goes back to antiquity. It has the advantage of being rather simple, and covered in most introductory physics courses. Moreover, it is a rather typical case of how scientific descriptions of natural phenomena evolve over time, starting with simple empirical models that are replaced with more explanatory ones as the understanding of the fundamental mechanisms improves. Finally, the computational techniques for dealing with these models are widely used for other applications in many fields of science. Readers with a background in chemistry or biology may not find Newton's equations particularly relevant for their work, but may find consolation in the fact that most of what I say about Newton's equations applies equally well to reaction rate equations or to the Lotka–Volterra equations.

The theory of computation has also made important contributions to the practice of science. A significant part of today's scientific knowledge is, or can be, formulated as algorithms. Algorithms in turn can be encoded as digital information, just like numbers or images. This creates new ways to analyze and reason about scientific knowledge. One application is the quantification of the complexity of scientific models and datasets, which permits one to distinguish in a mathematically precise way between regular and random phenomena, a distinction that lies at the heart of scientific modeling.

2.1 Traditional science: celestial mechanics

The apparent motion of the Sun, the Moon, and the planets in the sky has been the subject of intense observations and mathematical descriptions for millennia. Seen from Earth, these celestial bodies appear to move on two-dimensional paths, as their distance from Earth is not directly observable. People realized early that these paths are periodic, and approximately circular for many celestial bodies. Since the positions of the planets were believed to have a direct impact on events in daily life, there was a strong desire to be able to predict them. For this reason, astronomers started compiling tables of the observed positions of the major celestial bodies over time, and looking for regularities that allowed prediction.

2.1.1 Empirical models for planetary orbits

The position of each celestial body at a given time is specified in terms of two angular coordinates, the *azimuth* and the *altitude*, which depend on the location of the observer on the Earth's surface. In order to make predictions from such observations, it is necessary to construct an empirical mathematical model for them. In contrast to physical models, which I will discuss in the next section, such an empirical model is purely descriptive. It does not pretend to explain the observations, in the sense of identifying causes and underlying mechanisms. As a consequence, it does not permit answering 'what if' questions, such as 'how will the orbit of the Moon change if a heavy comet passes close to it?'

One of the most widely used empirical models for the solar system was introduced by Ptolemy in the 1st century. It describes the paths of all celestial bodies as circles around the Earth. Refinements were added over time, mainly in the form of *epicycles*: each planet moves on a small circle whose center moves on a large circle around the Earth, called a *deferent*, and assumed to be in the same plane as the epicycles. The speed of the motion along these curves is taken to be constant, and the orbits of all celestial bodies are considered as independent. Using modern notation, the parameters for such a model are (1) the radii R_i and the orbital periods T_i for each circle i, taking into account both deferents and epicycles, and (2) a reference angle $\phi_i(t_0)$ that defines the position on each circle at some reference time t_0.

From a computational point of view, this model is rather simple by today's standards. To compute a position at an arbitrary time t, one first computes $f_i(t) = (t - t_o)/T_i$, i.e. the fraction of the orbital period that has elapsed since the reference positions were observed. The next step is the computation of the angles $\phi_i(t) = \phi_i(t_0) + 2\pi f_i(t)$. Finally, the position of the body in its plane of motion can be expressed in terms of Cartesian coordinates $x(t) = \sum_i R_i \cos \phi_i(t)$, $y(t) = \sum_i R_i \sin \phi_i(t)$, where the summation is over the deferents and epicycles for the body. Assuming one deferent and one epicycle for a planet, the computation requires 14 elementary arithmetical operations and four evaluations of trigonometric functions, which can be replaced by lookups in precomputed tables.

Note that I have simplified this problem slightly. The astronomical coordinates, azimuth and altitude, are a bit more difficult to compute than Cartesian coordinates in a plane. Nevertheless, the computation of a planet's position in the sky remains limited to a small number of arithmetic operations and table lookups.

Variants of the empirical model described above remained in use until the 16th century. A significant improvement through simplification became possible only after Copernicus [1] revived the *heliocentric* model that had already been proposed in the 3rd century BCE by Aristarchus of Samos. Copernicus pointed out that the paths of the other celestial bodies appear complex only because we observe them from a moving viewpoint. Putting the Sun in the center of the solar system removed the need for epicycles: each planet's orbit around the Sun could be described by a single circle. This insight, coupled with significant progress in geometry, opened the way to rapid scientific progress: Kepler recognized the planetary orbits as elliptical rather than circular, and the velocities along the orbits as variable [2]. Shortly thereafter, Isaac Newton established a physical model [3] that could explain these elliptical orbits in terms of simple principles that also apply to objects in everyday life on Earth.

2.1.2 Newton's physical model

The step from empirical models to a physical model for planetary orbits was one of the most important transitions in the history of science. Newton's model for the solar system consists of two parts: the *laws of motion*, which describe how physical bodies move in reaction to forces, and the *law of universal gravitation*, which describes the forces acting between the bodies. From a philosophical point of view, this approach was revolutionary in two ways. First, it unified celestial and terrestrial physics, establishing universally valid principles. Second, it explained the motions of celestial bodies by a simpler and more fundamental underlying mechanism, rather than just describing their paths. As we will see, this second aspect is reflected in the computational nature of the model.

Newton's laws of motion state that the position $\mathbf{r}_i$ of each body $i = 1...N$ as a function of time is the solution of the differential equations

$$\frac{d}{dt}\mathbf{r}_i(t) = \mathbf{v}_i(t) \quad \mathbf{v}: \text{velocity}$$

$$\frac{d}{dt}\mathbf{v}_i(t) = \mathbf{a}_i(t) \quad \mathbf{a}: \text{acceleration} \tag{2.1}$$

$$\mathbf{F}_i(t) = m_i\mathbf{a}_i(t) \quad \mathbf{F}: \text{force}, m: \text{mass}$$

The law of universal gravitation specifies the forces acting on each body as

$$\mathbf{F}_i = \sum_{\substack{j=1\\j\neq i}}^{N} \mathbf{F}_{ij}$$

$$\mathbf{F}_{ij} = -G\frac{m_i m_j}{\left|\mathbf{r}_i - \mathbf{r}_j\right|^2}\frac{\mathbf{r}_i - \mathbf{r}_j}{\left|\mathbf{r}_i - \mathbf{r}_j\right|} \tag{2.2}$$

where G is a universal constant. Taken together, these equations fully determine the motion of all the bodies in the past and future. A specific assembly of celestial bodies, such as our solar system, is defined by a set of parameters, the masses m_i of all bodies. Moreover, since the laws of motion specify only *changes* in the positions and velocities, their values $\mathbf{r}_i(t_0)$ and $\mathbf{v}_i(t_0)$ at some time t_0 must be known as well.

Although a mathematical analysis of Newton's equations yields a proof that they specify the paths followed by the celestial bodies completely, it does not provide a recipe for actually computing numbers that could be compared to astronomical observations. This problem was already recognized by Newton, and has occupied scientists ever since. Today the mathematical and computational issues are well understood, but still present a challenge in practice.

For two celestial bodies, for example the Earth and the Sun, the equations given above have *analytical solutions*, i.e. solutions expressed in terms of elementary mathematical functions. For closed orbits (planets, as opposed to comets), they have exactly the elliptical form that Kepler had already derived empirically. Kepler's empirical model can thus be seen as the result of an approximation which consists of looking at each planet separately, taking into account only the interactions with the Sun. However, this approximation fails for one important celestial body: the Moon's orbit around the Earth is strongly influenced by the gravitational pull of both the Earth and the Sun, and requires an analysis of three interacting celestial bodies.

Significant efforts were undertaken to solve the 'three-body problem', as it soon became called, but nobody succeeded in finding an exact general solution. 200 years after Newton's work, Bruns and Poincaré showed that no general solution in terms of algebraic equations and integrals can exist. This does not exclude solutions expressed in terms of more sophisticated mathematical functions, but no such solution has been found to this day. Including more celestial bodies makes the problem only more difficult. In practice, the motion of celestial bodies can only be studied by making approximations to Newton's laws, and the only type of approximation that can be applied universally is a numerical solution of the equations of motion.

The term 'numerical solution' is probably familiar to most scientists, although it is not obvious what this term means exactly. A solution to equations (2.1) is a function $r_i(t)$ that specifies the position of body i at any time t. A numerical solution should then be a representation of this function in terms of numbers, either as a table or as an algorithm that performs the computation. Unfortunately, such a representation is impossible, because the components of the vectors r_i are real numbers. As I explained in section 1.1.2, a real number has infinite information content and can therefore not be written down, nor computed.

A 'numerical solution' is thus always an *approximate* solution expressed in terms of a subset of the real numbers that can be encoded in finite sequences of symbols. The best we could wish for as an approximate solution is an algorithm that, given two rational numbers t and ϵ, computes a position $\hat{r}_i(t)$ such that $|r_i(t) - \hat{r}_i(t)| < \epsilon$. The parameter ϵ is thus an upper limit on the error of the approximation. It is a little-known fact that such a solution algorithm can actually be constructed for Newton's equations of motion, even though this is not possible for differential equations in general [4]. I will explain the underlying ideas in more detail in section 3.6.3. Unfortunately, this approach is of little practical interest for studying the solar system, because the computational effort is prohibitive.

What is meant in practice by a numerical solution to Newton's equations is the result of three transformation steps:
1. The derivatives in the differential equations (2.1) are replaced by quotients of finite differences, e.g. $\mathrm{d}/\mathrm{d}t\, r_i(t)$ is replaced by $[r_i(t + \Delta t) - r_i(t)]/\Delta t$.
2. The finite-difference equations are rearranged to express $r_i(t + \Delta t)$ in terms of $r_i(t)$, allowing an iterative computation of the positions at t_0, $t_0 + \Delta t_1$, $t_0 + \Delta t_1 + \Delta t_2$, etc.
3. Arithmetic operations on real numbers are replaced by *floating-point arithmetic*, which inserts a rounding step after each operation.

Step 2 turns a *description* of the solution (an equation) into a recipe for its *construction* (an algorithm). This is possible only after step 1, an approximation that removes from the equations the limits-to-zero that are implicit in the derivatives. Step 3 introduces another approximation that reduces the computational effort. It is not strictly necessary to use floating-point arithmetic, but this is by far the most widely used approach today. I will discuss the problem of arithmetic in more detail in section 3.6.

The development and evaluation of approximations that permit the efficient computation of numerical solutions to mathematical equations has become a field of research of its own, called *numerical analysis*. For the planetary orbits in the solar system, numerical analysis has produced computational methods that are efficient and have predictable accuracy. To understand why this is a non-trivial achievement, consider that the computation of the planetary orbits is performed by following the motion of each body in many small steps. Even if the approximation error is small at each step, these errors accumulate over time. Moreover, the errors introduced by steps 1 and 3 interact in an unpleasant way. The error of step 1 can be reduced by choosing a smaller Δt, but then the errors due to rounding in step 3 become larger. In fact, efficient methods with predictable accuracy exist only for stable situations such as the periodic orbits of the solar system. When the same equations are applied to situations involving collisions or near-collisions of celestial bodies, computationally tractable methods have unknown accuracy, whereas methods with predictable accuracy require a prohibitive computational effort. This means that for such situations, known as 'chaotic dynamical systems', it is effectively impossible to verify the validity of Newton's equations, for purely computational reasons.

In the last section, we saw that the computation of the planets' positions in the sky at any given time using the empirical models of Ptolemy, Copernicus, or Kepler is a matter of a relatively small number of operations—let us say of the order of 100 for the whole solar system. Obtaining the same result from Newton's physical model requires a much more serious effort. Given the many existing variations on the algorithms for doing this computation, which differ in complexity, accuracy, and efficiency, it is not even obvious how to count the elementary operations that must be performed. This enormous difference in computational effort is characteristic for the difference between empirical and physical models. It is directly related to the fact that empirical models *describe* a specific phenomenon, and are thus 'close to the data', whereas physical models *explain* the phenomenon in terms of a more fundamental mechanism, requiring extensive computation to simulate the mechanism before a comparison with observed data becomes possible.

2.2 Scientific models and computation

After this case study of two different levels of description of the solar system, we can now look at different kinds of scientific models in a more general and abstract way, maintaining the focus on the computational aspects. This will allow us to see how recent computationally intensive models and methods fit into the picture, and how viewing scientific models as algorithms can help us in understanding their nature and their limitations.

Figure 2.1 shows a simplified overview of the roles of models and observations in scientific research. The parts of the research process in which computation plays an important role are highlighted in orange. What the figure describes is the process of exploring a single well-defined phenomenon using a single type of model. Scientific research as a whole consists of many such processes going on over time, with each one based on the insight obtained from many earlier studies. The big picture of science is a complex network in which each node resembles figure 2.1.

The starting point (top left) is the natural phenomenon that is the subject of study. It is explored experimentally by measurements (left column), leading to observed

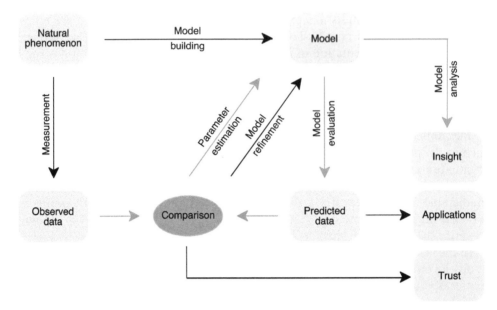

Figure 2.1. A simplified diagram of the process of scientific research. The green boxes show the 'output' of science: a model that is considered trustworthy after validation, the insight derived from it, and the possibility to use it in applications. The parts of the process that strongly depend on computation are shown in orange.

data. The right column represents the theoretical branch of science: mathematical and computational evaluation of a model produces theoretical predictions[1] for observable quantities, which are then compared to the outcome of measurements. Often the model has parameters that must be adjusted to the measurements. Any remaining discrepancy, assuming that it is not attributed to mistakes in the measurements, will give rise to a refinement of the model. Once the model is in sufficient agreement with the observations, i.e. once it is considered trustworthy for a certain application domain, further analysis can lead to insights into the original phenomenon beyond what could be deduced from the observed data alone.

Moreover, a trusted model can be used as a replacement for measurements, i.e. for predicting data that need not be checked any more. This is how scientific models are used in engineering, often replacing trial-end-error approaches to designing machines or buildings. There is of course no clear-cut distinction between science and engineering, as the transition from a hypothesis in need of validation to a trusted model happens slowly and continuously. Moreover, scientists regularly use engineering approaches based on trusted models for designing experimental equipment and computational procedures. From a computational point of view, the evaluation of a model is the same no matter if it is trusted or not. In the following, I will concentrate

---

[1] Some authors make a distinction between 'prediction' and 'postdiction', depending on whether the theoretical data are produced before or after the observation. This makes no difference for the computational aspects, so to keep the discussion simple I will always use the term 'prediction'.

on model evaluation in the context of validation, but keep in mind that almost everything can be applied to engineering-type uses as well.

The role of models in science is to formalize, most often by mathematical techniques, a description of patterns and regularities that have been detected in the phenomena being studied. The formalization of these descriptions is important to permit their precise and objective evaluation. A less obvious requirement is that the descriptions must be simpler than the observations that they describe. It is straightforward to construct a mathematical equation in such a way that a given set of numbers are solutions. However, such equations do not yield any insight, being no more than a reformulation of the data. The goal of a scientific model is to capture regularities yielding insight, and separate them from 'random' (i.e. irregular) contributions considered as 'noise' or 'errors'. This distinction was first formulated by Leibniz [5] in the 17th century, but the quantification of concepts such as 'simplicity', 'regularity', or 'randomness' became possible only with the theory of information and computation, as we will see in section 2.2.4.

In the case study of section 2.1; the development of both the empirical and the physical models can be analyzed in terms of this schema. The natural phenomenon is the motion of celestial bodies, and the measurements are astronomical observations. The model building step for the empirical models is based on data visualization (which is particularly straightforward in the case of visual observations) and trial-and-error guessing at a suitable mathematical form for the orbits: circles. Model evaluation, as I have explained above, consists of simple computations, as does the estimation of the model parameters. Model refinement happened over many centuries, as more and better observations became available. It consisted of adjusting the parameters of the circles, adding epicycles, and finally switching to a heliocentric coordinate system and then to elliptical orbits. The insight obtained from these models culminated in Kepler's three laws of planetary motion.

Newton's physical model was based on the insight derived from the earlier empirical models, combined with experience with terrestrial physics. Evaluation of the model is possible only using approximations, as I have explained above. Newton worked with the two-body approximation for the planetary orbits around the Sun, and a moderately successful perturbation approach for the orbit of the Moon around the Earth. Today, numerical approximations have become the standard tool, because they can take into account all interactions between a large number of bodies. This can be seen as a form of model refinement. The insight obtained from mathematical and computational analysis of the model is far too voluminous to summarize here: it fills many books. It includes general principles of mechanics, such as the conservation of energy. Among the applications of this model, the first notable one was the discovery of the planet Neptune, whose existence was first postulated theoretically in the 19th century, in order to explain deviations in the orbits of the already known planets. By this time, Newton's laws were already considered trustworthy enough that their validity was not questioned. Model refinement took the form of adding an entire planet.

Figure 2.1 highlights the importance of the comparison between observed data and predicted data, which serves to validate the model, to estimate values of its

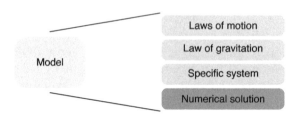

Figure 2.2. A closer look at the structure of Newton's physical model for celestial mechanics.

parameters and, if necessary, to refine it. The predicted data are obtained by model evaluation, which means computation. The immediate conclusion is that *every scientific model is an algorithm*. Obvious though this may be, it probably comes as a surprise to most scientists. The scientific literature, and in particular textbooks written for students, emphasizes the role of equations in scientific models, treating the process of finding a solution and computing predicted data as a technical detail. However, an equation is of use in science only if it can be solved, and it is its numerical solution that is validated by comparison with observed data. Another way to see the central role of algorithms is that there are scientific models that take the form of algorithms not founded on any equations (see section 2.2.5), but there are no cases of scientific models consisting of equations that cannot be solved at least approximately.

We can decompose Newton's model into distinct layers, shown in figure 2.2. At the top, we have the most general ingredient, the laws of motion, which describe a wide range of physical systems—in fact, until the beginning of the 20th century, they were believed to be universally valid for the dynamics of everything in the Universe. However, the laws of motion say nothing about the forces that enter into them. They must be specified separately, and for celestial mechanics that specification is the law of gravitation (second box). To describe a concrete physical system, we must moreover supply that system's numerical parameters (third box), i.e. the masses and initial positions of the bodies. These three layers define the complete equations of motion. The fourth layer on the bottom represents the algorithm that computes predicted data. As we have seen above, it is obtained from the top three layers by approximations. It is this bottom layer that is validated, but all four layers enter into the refinement cycle, and all four layers can be the starting point for model analysis yielding insight. For example, the top two layers are sufficient to derive conservation of energy, the top three layers permit an analysis of the stability of the solar system, but only the fourth layer can be used to answer 'what if' questions, such as exploring the perturbations caused by a comet. The top layer and its analysis is often called a *theory*, and the theory based on Newton's laws of motion is known today as *classical mechanics*.

2.2.1 Characterizing models by computational effort

In the celestial mechanics example of section 2.1 I have underlined the important difference between the empirical and physical models in terms of the computational effort required for model evaluation. Since all scientific models are algorithms, this notion can be generalized. Anticipating the use of a measure called *logical depth*, which I will introduce in section 2.2.4, I will call a scientific model *shallow* if it yields predicted data with few computational operations, and *deep* if many operations are required. We can then say that Newton's physical model is much deeper than the empirical models that preceded it. Deep models are of course inconvenient from a pragmatic point of view, because we need to invest more computational resources to make predictions. We therefore expect a deeper model to offer some advantages in return, compared to a more shallow model. For Newton's model, these advantages are generality, accuracy, and explanatory power.

Model validation, represented by the 'comparison' operation in figure 2.1, is a fundamental requirement of the scientific method. It is the reality check that distinguishes science from speculation. Model validation requires the availability of both observed and predicted data. It is therefore limited both by what can be measured and by what can be computed. The computational resources available to science thus impose a limit on the depth of useful scientific models. We might, for example, be tempted, for the sake of generality and explanatory power, to construct a model for the solar system at the atom level, using quantum mechanics as the underlying theory. Such a project is doomed to fail because we cannot solve the Schrödinger equation (the fundamental equation of quantum mechanics) for more than a few hundred atoms, even using severe and therefore inaccurate approximations. Moreover, computational complexity theory (the subject of section 3.5) suggests that even with more powerful computers we will probably never be able to study the whole solar system at the atom level. Fortunately, an atom level description of the solar system is also of little use in obtaining insight, because the wealth of detailed information about atomic motions hides the essential characteristics of planetary motions. The temptation to actually pursue such a level of description is therefore limited. Nevertheless, the idea of a single fundamental theory explaining all of nature remains popular, in particular among physicists, in spite of the fact that for reasons of computational complexity, it is likely to be forever impossible to validate a theory claiming to explain everything ranging in size from elementary particles to galaxies, and including complex assemblies of matter such as living organisms.

2.2.2 Empirical models: from linear regression to data science

Empirical modeling remains a cornerstone of science. It is, in particular, the first step in the scientific study of every new phenomenon. Empirical modeling starts with someone noticing patterns or regularities in observations, and trying to capture them mathematically. Note that 'mathematically' does not necessarily mean 'equations', although equations are the most common form of mathematical models for quantitative data. An example for non-quantitative models giving rise to non-equational models is the study of metabolic pathways in biochemistry, which are described by graphs. However, to keep the discussion focused, I will limit myself to quantitative models in this section.

Empirical modeling typically proceeds along the following pattern:
1. Inspection of the data, using visualization techniques such as plotting, in order to find an appropriate mathematical model.
2. Fitting the parameters of the model to the observed data.
3. Inspection of the deviations in the observed data from the model. Comparison with the known or estimated accuracy of the measurement techniques.
4. Use of additional observations to verify the model and to establish its domain of validity.

All of these steps involve a mixture of computation and human creativity and judgment. Human creativity is required for constructing an appropriate model[2], and human judgment applies in the decision if a model is good enough.

It is important to understand that all data analysis relies on models, and that the validity of these models must always be evaluated with a critical attitude. Some empirical models are so simple or so familiar that we can easily forget that they are models, and that they might be inappropriate. For example, performing linear regression on a dataset means applying a model that is based on two assumptions: (1) the relation between the two variables is linear, and (2) the measurement errors follow a normal distribution with identical parameters for all data points. A scientist applying linear regression is usually aware of the first assumption, which is part of the name of the procedure, but can easily forget the second one. The occasional description of data analysis procedures as 'model-free' also suggests that scientists often fail to recognize the models, and thus the assumptions, underlying their data processing protocols.

The insight that can be obtained from empirical models is often limited to the fact that the model describes the data. Additional insight can be derived from a study of the fitted parameters, which may themselves show regularities when compared across different observation datasets. An example from celestial mechanics is Kepler's third law, which results from a comparison of the orbital parameters of different planets.

Computers have revolutionized data analysis with empirical models in several ways. First of all, they can process far larger datasets. Second, they can handle much more complex mathematical models. Third, they can rapidly re-do computations to take into account new observations. While points one and three are generally beneficial for the quality of data analysis procedures, point two is a double-edged sword. More complex models can describe a wider range of phenomena, but they also make it more difficult to derive insight, which, as figure 2.1 shows, is one the primary outputs of scientific research. Moreover, the ease with which complex models can be applied using ready-made computer software often turns their use into a technical routine from which all critical judgment is eliminated. An example that has caused much debate in recent years is the routine application of complex statistical analysis procedures in medical research, where the criteria for the validity

---

[2] See the end of section 2.3.1 for the still marginal technique of automated model discovery.

of the analysis are usually not checked, and in retrospect often turn out not to be satisfied [6].

A recent development is the use of very general models with many parameters, which by design can fit almost any dataset. The best known models of this kind are *artificial neural networks*. Such models are associated with automated parameter fitting algorithms that can process large datasets of unknown nature, requiring little or no human input. These methods are collectively referred to as *machine learning* approaches. After a learning phase on a training dataset, the resulting parametrized model can be used for making predictions. Very similar statistical models are also employed with the goal of detecting patterns in large datasets, in an approach known as *data mining* or *knowledge extraction*. The term 'machine learning' is used when the emphasis is on using the trained model for making predictions, whereas the term 'data mining' is preferred when the focus is on deriving insight from a study of the fitted parameters. These techniques have had some spectacular successes in engineering applications such as machine translation or computer vision. Their use in data analysis, in combination with more traditional methods of statistics, is called *data science*. In the context of scientific research, the main difficulty is generating insight from a large parameter set, in which no clear meaning can be attributed *a priori* to the individual parameters. For now, machine learning and data mining are used to support rather than replace human experts in the analysis of complex datasets.

As I have explained earlier, the role of a scientific model is to capture regularities in observations and separate them from random 'errors'. The size of the observed data must therefore be much larger than the number of parameters that are being adjusted. Data science thus requires huge input datasets and as a consequence significant computational resources. Nevertheless, like all empirical models, the models of data science are shallow. The computational effort is due to the size of the datasets and the complexity of the parameter fitting or learning process. The evaluation of the resulting model, for example an artificial neural network, for one set of input data, remains a simple task involving few computational operations.

2.2.3 Explanatory models: from simple to complex systems

Explanatory models differ from empirical models in describing the natural phenomenon being studied at a more fundamental level, providing an explanation of the phenomenon instead of only a description. As the case study of celestial mechanics has shown, explanatory models have significant advantages: they are more general, explaining a wide variety of situations, and they provide more insight into the processes at work. Generality also has the indirect benefit of permitting more validation and thus higher trust in the model. In the example, Newton's laws of motion can be validated by studying falling stones or moving trains in addition to planetary orbits. On the other hand, the higher computational depth of an explanatory model makes them more difficult to apply and limits the size and complexity of the systems for which they can be validated.

The evaluation of explanatory models is generally called a *simulation*. Before electronic computers, it was too laborious to be performed numerically except for very simple systems. Today, simulation techniques are one of the main uses of computing in scientific research as well as in engineering. As for the case of empirical models, the size and complexity of simulations has increased enormously over the few decades that computers have been available to scientists.

In celestial mechanics simulations, the output of the simulation is the planetary orbits over some period of time. This information is very close to the observed data that astronomers obtain with their telescopes. All it takes to convert planetary orbits in a Cartesian coordinate system to azimuth–altitude pairs is a coordinate transformation. While the derivation of this transformation is tricky, its computational evaluation is trivial. This also means that verifying the accuracy and refining the model (e.g. by fine-tuning its parameters) is rather straightforward.

In contrast, many of today's scientific simulations have *complex systems* as their subject of study. A complex system is defined as a system that has relevant observable properties that its constituents do not have, and which are therefore called *emergent properties*. For example, a water molecule has vibrational frequencies, observable by spectroscopy, that do not exist in hydrogen or oxygen atoms. At the next level of organization, liquid water has properties such as density or viscosity, which do not make sense for a single water molecule. Different levels of complexity in the structure of matter have traditionally been handled by different scientific models. The interactions of the nuclei and electrons of hydrogen and oxygen atoms that shape the properties of a water molecule are described within the theory of quantum mechanics, whereas the behavior of liquid water is described in the frameworks of thermodynamics and fluid dynamics. Before computers, bridging two or more levels of description was limited to particularly simple cases or required drastic approximations. Computer simulations have turned this into an almost routine task. They make it possible to *compute* properties such as the viscosity of liquid water by an explicit simulation of the interactions of many individual water molecules. This has led to new ways to construct, validate, and refine scientific models, but also to new types of approximations, which are introduced to keep the computational resources required by such simulations at a manageable level.

Let us look at the water example in more detail. In principle, all the properties of a water molecule are determined by the solution of the Schrödinger equation for two hydrogen atoms and one oxygen atom, where each atom is described by its nucleus and its electrons. However, no analytical solution is known for this system. Quantum chemistry has developed sophisticated approximations that allow very accurate numerical computations of molecular properties for water and other molecules, up to the size of about a hundred atoms. It is therefore also possible to study clusters of water molecules with a similar accuracy as single molecules. However, the macroscopic properties of liquid water require a much larger number of molecules. As an illustration, a raindrop contains about 10^{20} water molecules. Moreover, the larger size of the system to consider also introduces longer time scales that must be simulated. The slowest motions in a water molecule are bending vibrations, whose oscillation period is about 170 ps. The slowest molecular motion in a raindrop is the diffusion of a water molecule across the drop, which takes a few hours. Quantum chemistry simulations of a raindrop are therefore clearly out of the reach of today's computers.

A typical simulation of water and other molecular liquids relies on two approximations, both of which were specifically developed for simulations. First, the macroscopic sample (our raindrop) is replaced by a small cell, typically of cubic shape for simplicity, containing a few hundred molecules. This cell is surrounded by identical copies of itself, repeated periodically in space. The atoms in all the periodic images of the cell move together, meaning that only the few hundred atoms in a single cell need to be simulated explicitly. This approximation yields a small and thus tractable system that does not have any surface. The small size of the cell limits the phenomena that can be studied. Its choice represents a compromise between computational effort and utility of the results. Second, the interactions among the hydrogen and oxygen atoms are described by empirical models that replace the explanatory quantum-mechanical one. Such empirical models resemble the ones described in section 2.2.2; but differ in one very important point: they are validated and refined not only by comparison with observed data, but also with simulations performed with the more fundamental and more accurate quantum chemistry model. The main motivation for introducing these empirical models is to reduce computational complexity by replacing a deep model by a shallow one. The combined use of multiple models at different levels is known as *multiscale modeling*, and is illustrated in figure 2.3. It has become an essential tool in both materials science and the life sciences. The combination of models at different scales can take several forms First, the higher-level models are often calibrated using the lower-level ones, as in the example I have given for water models. Second, different parts of a system can be described at different levels, 'zooming in' on a specific region with a detailed model, while handling the bulk of the system with a computationally cheaper one. Third, a single simulation can alternate between two different scales, for example to compute slow changes with a higher-level model and faster ones using a more detailed one.

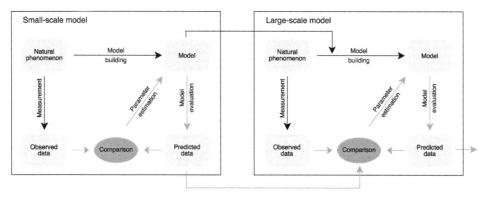

Figure 2.3. Multiscale modeling: Two (or more) different models describe the same physical system at different length and time scales. The small-scale model also serves as a source of reference data for calibrating the large-scale model.

Another approach for describing complex systems is *multiphysics simulation*. The traditional mathematical models for the dynamical processes occurring in matter are distinct equations for each type of process. Diffusion, flow, wave propagation, or chemical kinetics are each described by a specific differential equation. In many real-life situations, several such processes occur together. For example, a chemical reaction can take place in a flowing liquid. Coupling the required equations is not fundamentally difficult, but leads to complex and often non-linear systems of equations for which numerical approaches are the only viable ones.

The simulation of complex systems has created some confusion concerning the role of simulation in scientific research. Any simulation approach introduces problems such as finite accuracy and statistical errors, which are traditionally associated with experiments rather than theory. Moreover, the construction of empirical models based on simulations of lower-level explanatory models uses the same mathematical techniques as the construction of empirical models for observed data. Some scientists therefore see simulations as a form of experiment performed on a computer, and describe them using terms such as 'computational microscopes' that suggest a similarity to experimental instruments. However, simulations remain fully on the theoretical right-hand branch of figure 2.1. They explore models, not natural phenomena. The use of terminology from experimental science makes it easy to forget the models that are applied, and that need to be validated before any conclusions can be drawn from them.

Another factor that hides the fundamental role of models in simulations is the complexity of many empirical models that makes them difficult to formulate precisely in scientific publications. In the example of liquid water that I have used above, the empirical models are simple enough to be described by a few equations with a small number of parameters. For example, a popular water model called TIP3P [7] involves three simple interaction terms and six numerical parameters. Applying the exact same approach to proteins, however, yields models with hundreds of numerical parameters and non-trivial algorithms that construct a list of interaction terms by analyzing a graph describing the molecular structure. Such models are difficult to describe in scientific publications because neither human languages nor mathematical formulas nor tables of numbers can express all their ingredients. The only complete and precise formulations of these models are written in programming languages and are part of the simulation software that applies them. Simulation software is written with a focus on efficient execution, rather than on ease of understanding by human readers, which makes it a bad medium for documenting scientific models. Many of today's computational models for complex systems are therefore obscure to the point that their users do not even try to understand them. Moreover, models that are integral parts of simulation software cannot be validated independently of that software. But software changes at a fast pace, dictated by the evolution of computing technology. Today's version of software package X may well implement a slightly different model than last year's version, either intentionally in the course of model refinement, or as the result of mistakes made in software development. It is therefore difficult to find out how some exact version of a model, as implemented in a piece of software, has been validated.

Unfortunately, we do not have a satisfactory solution to these problems at this time. Nevertheless, many useful partial solutions have been identified, and are discussed in section 4.4 and chapter 5. In chapter 7, I will outline what remains to be done.

2.2.4 Measuring the complexity of a model

When studying complex systems using computers, it is important to distinguish the complexity of an observed phenomenon from the complexity of the model used to describe it. Explanatory models for complex systems are in general simple, meaning that they can be written down in a compact form that scientists can conveniently work with. Quantum chemistry describes even complex molecules by a fundamentally simple model, although this simplicity is somewhat hidden by the non-trivial approximations that must be made in order to obtain numerical results efficiently. On the other hand, empirical models for complex molecules are complex themselves, having such a large number of parameters that it is no longer possible to manipulate them without the help of computers.

One of the principles in the construction of scientific models, often called 'Occam's Razor', is a search for simplicity. If a set of observations can be explained by more than one model, the pragmatic choice is to go with the simplest one, because it is both easier to validate and easier to understand. However, it is not at all evident what simplicity means. One could count the number of terms in an equation, for example, or the number of numerical parameters. Such heuristic metrics are sufficient for eliminating approaches that are 'obviously' too complicated, but they do not answer all the relevant questions. Newton's law of gravitation (equation 2.2) specifies the force between two celestial bodies as $F = G\frac{m_1 m_2}{r}^2$. But Newton could equally well have chosen $r^{1.9999}$ instead of r^2. Most physicists would intuitively prefer an integer power, like Newton did. Can this intuition be explained based on mathematical principles? Can it be generalized to much more complex models, for which our intuition fails?

If we formulate our models as computer programs, we can begin to explore these questions systematically. Two computer programs can in principle be compared objectively, for example by measuring their lengths and their run time. Anyone who has ever written a non-trivial computer program will immediately raise some objections to this idea, and indeed there are many pitfalls. Comparing program lengths makes sense only for programs written in the same language. They should not include any comments, and the impact of arbitrary choices such as variable naming must be eliminated. A more serious problem is the cost of abstraction (see section 5.3.4), which makes non-trivial programs longer and slower than strictly necessary because of the structure that must be maintained to ensure that human brains can manage them. However, these difficulties can be overcome at least for simple programs, and the formal models of computation discussed in chapter 3 permit the definition of usable metrics for program length and run time. They show, for example, that the computation of r^2, which is a simple multiplication, is both much shorter to write and much quicker to compute than $r^{1.999}$, whose evaluation requires a logarithm and an exponentiation in addition to a multiplication by a constant. Integer powers are thus simpler than non-integer powers in an objective sense.

The same approach can be used to measure the information content and complexity of datasets, by introducing one additional idea: the use of a computer program as a description of its output. This is the starting point of *algorithmic information theory*. We consider a piece of data, no matter where it comes from, as the result of a computation, and we look for the shortest computer program that produces our data as output. The length of this program is a measure for the information content of our data and is called its *Kolmogorov complexity*. Some examples may help to illustrate this concept. Take the character string 'aaaaaaaaaa', i.e. ten times the letter 'a', occupying ten bytes of memory[3]. In the Python language, it can be computed as 10*'a'. That is one byte for 'a', four bits for 10, plus some value uniquely identifying the multiplication operation, altogether less than ten bytes. Likewise, the character string 'abababababab' can be shortened to 5*'ab'. But 'Maevih4aAi' cannot be computed from some smaller data in any obvious way. In fact, the Kolmogorov complexity is highest for completely random data. In the absence of any regularity that could be exploited in a computation, the shortest program contains the data as part of its source code and simply reproduces them as its output. Algorithmic information theory actually *defines* random data as data that cannot be produced by a program that is significantly shorter than its output. This definition is very similar in spirit to the separation of regularities from errors in the construction of a scientific model (see section 2.2).

The Kolmogorov complexity of a dataset is an interesting theoretical concept, but it has the practical disadvantage that its computation is impossible. The reason is that there is no way to prove that any given computer program is the shortest one that produces the required output. At first sight, this should be possible at least in principle, by generating all programs shorter than the given one, and running them to check if they produce the same output. The problem is that some of the generated programs will never stop!

However, useful approximations to Kolmogorov complexity can be defined and have been used in data analysis tasks. The basic idea is to describe the dataset using some language that is less powerful than a full programming language, but in exchange permits the identification of the smallest possible description (see section 3.4). This is known as the *minimal description length* approach (see [8] for an introduction to this and related concepts in the context of scientific models). One possible choice for such a restricted language is a data compression method, with the language being implemented by the decompression program.

It is also interesting to consider the execution time of the shortest program that produces a given dataset, which is known as the data's *logical depth*. Data with a high logical depth are the result of many steps of computation, resulting in intricate relations between their elements. A high logical depth makes it difficult to find the data-generating program, because this means effectively doing the computation in

---

[3] I am simplifying this a bit for pedagogical purposes. Character strings need more storage because some length indicator is required.

reverse. There is no fundamental relation between the Kolmogorov complexity of a dataset and its logical depth, just as a computer program's length permits no conclusion about its run time.

Algorithmic information theory is not directly concerned with scientific models. In particular, it does not address the problem of deriving insight from a computational description of measurements, nor the common goal in science to find general models that are transferable to many different situations. Nevertheless, the concepts and techniques developed in algorithmic information theory can be applied to the evaluation of scientific models, in particular when formulated as algorithms. I started this section by noting that a complex phenomenon can result from a simple, usually explanatory model, or from a complex empirical model. In the first case, the complexity in the behavior of the system comes from logical depth, in the second case, it is reflected by the Kolmogorov complexity of the model. The application of Occam's Razor as it is understood today resembles the search for the shortest program in the definition of Kolmogorov complexity. However, Occam's Razor is ultimately a pragmatic criterion for choosing the most useful model to work with. Computational cost is more and more becoming a criterion for evaluating scientific models, and it is quite possible that future generations of scientists will redefine the simplicity in Occam's Razor as some combination of Kolmogorov complexity and logical depth.

2.2.5 Getting rid of the equations

What I have described up to here is the most widespread use pattern of computation in science. It remains particularly common in the physical sciences. Their foundational theories are old, ranging from Newton's classical mechanics in the 17th century to quantum mechanics in the 1920s, and thus predate both electronic computers and the theory of computation. These theories are formulated as differential equations that have exact analytical solutions only for a very small number of applications. For everything else, computational models are derived from the differential equations through a few approximation steps, as I have shown in section 2.1.2.

Since in the end all scientific models must be formulated as algorithms if we want to compare with observations, do we need the differential equations at all? The answer is no: nothing in figure 2.1 requires differential equations. A computer program that computes predictions for some observations is a perfectly good scientific model. It does not matter if the program was derived from some equations or not.

Indeed we see more and more scientific models that are directly formulated in terms of algorithms. This development is most visible today in the life sciences, which study natural phenomena that are much more complex than anything physicists or chemists could ever handle within their traditional theories. Some modeling approaches from the physical sciences, including computational ones, have been successfully applied in the study of living systems. The atomic structure of biological molecules (proteins, DNA, RNA, lipids) is studied using the same simulation methods that were initially developed for much smaller molecules. Blood flow is described by the same techniques of computational fluid dynamics as microfluidic devices. But other phenomena in living organisms are not straightforward applications of physics and chemistry, and even for some that are, the higher complexity of the systems makes traditional approaches impossible to apply or practically useless.

As an example, let us look at protein interaction networks in cells. A cell consists of cytoplasm surrounded by a membrane. The cytoplasm contains many different molecules, among which there are thousands of different types of proteins. These proteins and their interactions form a sophisticated information processing network. The individual steps in these interactions are chemical reactions, in particular chemical modifications of proteins in specific places. In principle, these processes could be described just like chemical reactions in a test tube, i.e. by differential equations for the concentrations of each molecular species. But the number of molecular species is much too large to apply such an approach, as each distinct modification of each protein counts as a different molecule. More importantly, such an approach would not yield any insight into how cells process information. It would yield as a result the concentrations of each protein variant as a function of time. But what matters in an interaction network is specific sequences of reactions, known as signaling pathways, and not the dynamics of each type of step in such a sequence.

An alternative and much more productive approach is to describe signaling pathways as chains of events with probabilities assigned to each type of event. An interaction network is represented by a graph, and changes in the network are described by graph rewrite rules [9; 10]. The evolution of the network can then be studied by stochastic simulation, which consists of repeatedly applying randomly chosen rules. But stochastic simulation is only one technique in the study of these networks. For example, a combinatorial analysis of the graphs and rules provides insight into possible signaling paths. Given the size and complexity of the interaction graphs, none of these explorations would be possible without electronic computers.

This example is typical for what distinguishes the study of complex systems from the isolated study of physical and chemical processes inside such a system. The most detailed characterization of the individual processes in a cell is a theoretical model for how each process occurs in a test tube. This is traditional chemistry, with its reaction-rate based models. For understanding how a cell works, a precise description of the chemistry is much less relevant than a description of how thousands of reactions are coordinated. Complex systems require very different models because the questions being asked are very different.

A similar situation arises in the physical sciences when studying emergent phenomena in complex systems. A characteristic feature of emergent phenomena is that they do not depend on all the details of the interactions between the individual constituents of the system. This is in fact what made their scientific study possible at all before large-scale computer simulations were possible. It is also the reason why multiscale modeling works. The fact that liquids undergo viscous flow, whereas solids react to external forces by elastic deformation, is a consequence of the fundamental differences in the atomic structures of liquids and solids, but does not depend on the details of the specific atomic and molecular interactions. Physicists have always studied such phenomena using 'toy models', i.e. models that are simplified to the point of not even trying to represent any concrete real system. The predictions that toy models make about observations are therefore often not quantitative but only qualitative. Traditional toy models are developed within the framework of the standard theories based on differential equations, e.g. hard-sphere models for liquids. More recent approaches have used toy models that are defined computationally, e.g. cellular automata [11], which allow larger simulations because the individual computational steps are much simpler.

Since purely computational models are possible, could *all* scientific models perhaps be formulated that way? We could then relegate the old differential equations to the archives of scientific libraries, and start from scratch with a new algorithmic approach. Another way to phrase this question is whether the traditional theories of physics were formulated as differential equations for some fundamental reason, or just by historical accident. One motivation for this line of research is pragmatic. As I have explained in section 1.1.2, it is impossible to compute with real numbers because each real number has infinite information content. Computable models must therefore be derived from the original equations using approximations from numerical analysis. A direct formulation of a theory in terms of computation would eliminate one layer of formalism (the equations) and at least one layer of approximations.

However, to this day, nobody has come up with a credible computational replacement for any of the established physical theories, because real numbers are of fundamental importance for geometry and calculus. In fact, the concept of real numbers was developed in the context of geometry. Greek mathematicians knew already more than 2000 years ago that simple geometrical quantities such as the ratios of the lengths of the sides of a triangle cannot be represented by rational numbers. The irrational nature of π, and thus of many geometrical quantities related to circles, was shown only in the 18th century, which also saw the development of calculus. The concept of real numbers was shaped during this process, culminating in Cantor's rigorous set-theoretic definition. Cantor also discovered that the set of real numbers is not countable, which is the reason why they cannot be used in computation. The infinities associated with real numbers and calculus were always recognized as a practical difficulty, but taken as a sign of the divine nature of the laws of the Universe, for which human computational capabilities were only an imperfect match.

Renouncing real numbers thus means giving up on 2000 years of developments in geometry and calculus, which are not easily replaced by new foundations. A Universe described in terms of discrete rather than continuous variables cannot be isotropic, nor contain exact triangles. One line of research [4; 12] attempts to reformulate geometry and calculus in terms of *computable numbers*, which I will explain in section 3.6. If successful, it would solve at least some of the philosophical issues, and perhaps ultimately lead to better numerical techniques as well.

2.3 Computation at the interface between observations and models

A key element of the scientific process shown in figure 2.1 is the comparison of observed data and the corresponding predictions from a model. Very frequently, a model has some numerical parameters for which there are no *a priori* values. These parameters are therefore adjusted to make the model match the observations as closely as possible. For example, in Ptolemy's model for the solar system, the trajectories of all celestial bodies were assumed to be circles around Earth, but the radii of the circles and the angular position of each body at some initial time were not assumed nor deduced, but adjusted to match the observations.

In many situations, the comparison step is not as straightforward as figure 2.1 suggests. One reason is that observations in general do not directly measure properties of the natural phenomena that are being studied. The measured values depend both on the system being observed and on the instruments used for the observation. Another reason is that the raw observations are sometimes inconvenient to use, or not accessible at all. Much modern experimental equipment performs data preprocessing, usually with the goal of reducing its size, and therefore does not provide the raw data. Finally, scientific models are designed to capture the regularities in observed data, but it is admitted that there are always 'errors', i.e. small discrepancies due to effects that are unknown, insufficiently well understood, or considered uninteresting.

2.3.1 Matching models and measurements

Let us look again at the celestial mechanics example of section 2.1. Newton's equations define the planetary orbits in terms of a few parameters: the masses of all the celestial bodies, and their positions and velocities at some fixed time t_0. The model makes no predictions for these parameters. Moreover, none of these parameters is directly observable. The equations also contain a universal parameter, the gravitational constant G. We need to determine the values of all these parameters from the observations that we have. This is a simple case of an *inference problem*; we will look at more complicated cases later. A model that must be completed by information from observations is called a *parametric model*. Most scientific models are parametric.

The main difficulty in our inference problem is that we cannot solve Newton's equations without making approximations. We will first consider the physical approximation of an isolated two-body system, such as the Earth moving around the Sun. The exact solution of this approximated problem is an elliptical orbit of the Earth around the Sun[4]. While the derivation of the required mathematical formulas is not a trivial task [13], the subsequent computation of the Earth's trajectory around the Sun, and of the associated astronomical observables (azimuth and altitude of the Sun's apparent path in the sky), for a given set of model parameters, is

---

[4] More precisely, both the Earth and the Sun move along an elliptical orbit around their center of mass, but since the Sun's mass is so much larger, it is a good approximation (yet another one!) to say that the Earth moves around the Sun.

straightforward. We can then consider these mathematical relations as a set of equations that define the unknown model parameters, and look for a solution.

The remaining problem to be solved is how to deal with the errors. Astronomical observations are not perfect, and the model we are considering (the elliptical orbit) is not perfect either. We thus cannot expect to find any parameter set that solves the equations exactly. The only way to make progress is to make some assumptions about the errors of both model and observations, i.e. introduce an *error model*. Fortunately, if the errors are small enough, the precise characteristics of the error model do not matter. The most popular error model for such situations is the *Gaussian error model* which assumes that each observation has a random error that follows a normal distribution with zero mean, that the errors of all observations are independent, and that the widths of all normal distributions are the same. The Gaussian error model leads directly to the *least-squares fit* approach to determining model parameters. It is computationally trivial for models that are linear in their parameters. In that case, a unique best parameter set exists, and can be computed using efficient algorithms. For non-linear models, the problem becomes much harder: finding a solution requires additional approximations and computationally more expensive algorithms, and solutions are not guaranteed to be unique.

For the purpose of parameter fitting, there is no fundamental difference between shallow, i.e. empirical, and deep, i.e. explanatory, models. As long as the model can be evaluated for a fixed set of numerical parameter values, least-squares fitting can be applied. However, there is a difference in practice because empirical models can often be *constructed* to be linear in their parameters, whereas this option is almost never available for explanatory models. In fact, the higher logical depth of an explanatory model means that there is no simple relation between a change in the model and the impact of this change on the model's predictions. This leaves little room for arbitrary choices such as linearity—which is exactly the reason why explanatory models yield more insight into the laws of nature.

A very frequent situation is that the observed data are insufficient to fully define all numerical parameters in a model. In extreme cases, this suggests that the model was not well chosen. If we try to estimate the Moon's diameter from its orbit around Earth, we will not get very far because the orbits of celestial bodies do not depend on their diameters. However, in many situations the observed data provide *some* information about model parameters, but not enough to compute unique values. We can then try to quantify the uncertainty in the model parameters that remains after we have used all the available data. The most widely used approach to this is *Bayesian inference*, which is based on a quantification of uncertainties by probability distributions. For each parameter in our model, we have a distribution that incorporates all the knowledge we have about it. Initially that may be very little, such as knowing that a parameter must be positive. Each data point from observation then adds further information, which is combined with the prior information using Bayes' rule from probability theory. In the end, we have the so-called *posterior* probability distribution, which sums up what we know about our parameters. Like least-squares parameter fitting, Bayesian inference only requires that we can evaluate the model for given values of the parameters. However, the computational effort for performing Bayesian inference is much more important, to the point that it has become a practically applicable tool only about 20 years ago.

What I have discussed until now is the most frequent situation in which the parameters to be adjusted are numbers. A parameter could also represent a mathematical function, or a graph. The most general form that a parameter can take is a computational algorithm. As we have seen above, a complete scientific model is itself a computational algorithm. A parameter is thus a kind of sub-model. Procedures that identify non-numerical parameters are therefore sometimes called *automated model discovery* methods [14]. They require two ingredients. First, a representation that can express all possible values of the parameters in terms of data structures in a computer program. Second, a search algorithm that explores the space of possible parameter values and identifies the best match with the available measurements. The search procedures are usually *heuristic*, meaning that they cover only a part of parameter space. Often such search procedures are based on the principle of *genetic algorithms*, which emulate the optimization process in natural evolution. A recent example is the computational identification of a regulatory network in flatworms that is responsible for the regeneration of tissues after injuries [15]. Automated model discovery shares many features with the statistical models used in machine learning and data mining. In particular, the part of the model that is imposed by the designer of the method is very general. In contrast to traditional scientific models, the role of this pre-defined part is not to formalize scientific hypotheses, but to define a manageable search space for parameter estimation.

2.3.2 Mixing models and measurements

In the last section, I have discussed the common situation of a mathematical model having numerical parameters that are determined from measured data. In fact, most quantities that we call 'measurements' are strictly speaking parameters fitted to a model for the instrument that was used in the experiment. As a simple example, consider a spring scale used for measuring forces. What is really measured is the elongation of the spring. The force is deduced from the elongation using the known characteristics of the spring—in other words, a model for the spring. A more complex example is given by the fundamental physical constants (the gravitational constant G, the speed of light in vacuum c, etc), which are obtained by parameter estimation from a combination of many measurements and models connecting them [16].

We tend to consider such values as 'obtained by experiment', in spite of the fact that they depend on the choice of a specific model describing the experimental setup. Their classification as experimental data is justified if the major source of uncertainty for their values is the limited precision of the measurements. This implies that the underlying model is trusted and that the measurements fully determine the values of the model parameters.

With the large and complex models that have been made possible by electronic computers, these assumptions are not always justified. Such models are more difficult to validate, and they are therefore only partially trustworthy. Moreover, sophisticated inference procedures can handle incomplete measurements, yielding parameter values with large uncertainties even if each individual experimental input is very precise. Insufficiently validated models and insufficient measurements are sources of uncertainty that must be clearly distinguished from the uncertainty that is due to limited experimental precision.

A good example is given by the atomic structures for proteins that are obtained by x-ray crystallography. A crystallography experiment does not measure atomic positions, but only averages over distances between atom pairs. For simple crystals, with few atoms in the unit cell, this information is sufficient to reconstruct the atomic positions. For the many thousand atoms in the unit cell of a typical protein crystal, this is not possible. Protein structures are obtained by constructing a model that takes into account the chemical structure of the molecule. The parameters of this model are then obtained in an inference procedure from the measurements. The model parameters include the atom positions, but also additional parameters introduced to describe disorder in the crystal. Moreover, the model is based on assumptions known not to be satisfied, such as the statistical independence of individual measurement values. The final published atomic structures are thus influenced by model errors and defects of the inference procedures, and can therefore not be treated as simple observations on proteins.

A clear understanding of how measurements and observations contribute to the values of model parameters is particularly important in the context of computerized instruments that deliver preprocessed rather than raw measurements. Preprocessed data are in most cases parameters fitted to some model. But since the preprocessing happens automatically, without any explicit action by the scientist collecting the data, it can easily go unnoticed. Moreover, the instrument manufacturer does not necessarily provide a sufficient description of the model for judging its well-foundedness. This is another situation where models, which ought to be at the heart of scientific research, disappear inside computer software and thereby escape from the scrutiny they deserve.

2.4 Computation for developing insight

As figure 2.1 shows, the two main applications of models in science are making predictions and developing insight. Up to here, I have mainly discussed the first aspect. Deriving insight from a model is a less clearly defined process. Insight can be obtained in many ways, such as studying a model theoretically, or making modifications to it and exploring their consequences. Computation is not strictly required in this process, except when complex computational models are involved. Nevertheless, in practice computational methods play a big and ever growing role.

Perhaps the most widespread use of computers for developing insight is visualization. This can range from preparing a simple data plot to the generation of synthetic movies illustrating a complex physical process, and the data being visualized can come from measurements or from simulations. Many computational techniques collectively labeled as 'data analysis' play a similar role as visualization and are in fact often closely integrated with visualization methods. Examples are clustering or dimension reduction methods. The distinction between data analysis methods and scientific models is not always immediately obvious, although the basic principle is simple: a scientific model makes predictions that can be tested by comparison with observations. The computation of a quantity that cannot be measured cannot be part of a scientific model. This is the case for clusters in datasets, for example.

Another approach on the borderline between the construction of models and methods is the use of poorly validated or completely unvalidated models for hypothesis generation. The questions that are explored are 'what kind of observable can I predict with such a model?' or 'what kind of experiment would be useful to get more information about this phenomenon?' Computation is thus used for preparing more detailed theoretical or experimental work. The underlying idea is the same as with the use of 'toy models' by physicists that I discussed in section 2.2.5: when trying to understand general mechanisms, it is not necessary to have precise or realistic models for concrete physical systems.

In the life sciences, the use of computation for generating insight is perhaps even more important than for developing models. What sets life apart from other physical processes is evolution. The huge diversity of life forms that we observe is the result of millions of years of accumulated historical accidents. While there are some regularities in this diversity that can be captured in models, much of the information we have about living organisms cannot be explained but only be organized in a way that makes processing this information easier for humans. Much of bioinformatics, for example the computation of sequence alignments or phylogenetic trees, is dedicated to such an organization of information. Neither sequence alignments nor phylogenetic trees are observables, they are just useful concepts for human understanding. Similar needs for organization and classification exist at other levels. In structural biology, the concept of protein secondary structure is very important although it is just a classification of patterns in the atomic structure.

The predominance of data organization and analysis at least in the early days of bioinformatics has lead to an emphasis on 'method development' in which the question of whether or not a computed quantity is observable has become unimportant. As a consequence, a bioinformatician is more likely to work on a 'method to predict protein folding' than on a 'model for protein folding', although protein structures are observables (with the caveats described in section 2.3.2). This is not just a question of terminology. A bioinformatician will happily consider a stochastic method for predicting protein folding, and evaluate its probability for succeeding. In contrast, a physicist working on protein folding would insist that a model for this process must be deterministic in order to be a testable source of insight into the underlying process. Similar cultural differences are the root of the distinction between machine learning and data mining that I explained in section 2.2.2. It is quite possible that the increasing dependence of the physical and life sciences on computer science with its engineering culture will further blur the distinction between scientific models and computational methods.

2.5 The impact of computing on science

In the course of this chapter, I have pointed out the changes that computers have brought to scientific research. Some of these changes are direct consequences of the use of computers as tools, whereas others result from theoretical work in computer science and information theory that was motivated by the use of computers. It is worth summarizing these changes again in order to provide a compact overview:

Emergent properties of complex systems. Computer simulations make it possible to compute emergent properties of complex systems from a model describing its constituents, bridging different levels of description. The combination of these levels, known as multiscale modeling, has significantly increased the range of phenomena that can be studied by computer simulation. However, the validation of such simulations remains a challenge in many application domains.

Simulation replaces experiments. Computer simulations based on trusted models are often easier or cheaper to realize than experiments, and have therefore found an important role in engineering. In scientific research, simulations can help to reduce the number of experiments by careful preparation. The basic idea is to identify the most useful experimental conditions and parameters by prior simulation.

Confusion about the status of simulations. Computer simulations produce data that are similar in many respects to data obtained from measurements. Often the same techniques are used for further processing of the data. This has lead to a widespread confusion about the role of simulations in scientific research, with some scientists considering them a new kind of experiment rather than the exploration of a theoretical model.

Complex models. Computers can handle much more complex models than humans, with many more parameters. This has in particular permitted the construction of generic empirical models that can describe almost anything, but require huge datasets for parameter estimation. Such models have proven useful in engineering-type applications, but deriving scientific insight from them remains a challenge. Two problems shared by all complex computational models is that they are difficult to validate and difficult to publish in human-readable form.

Algorithms as scientific models. The necessity of computing numerical predictions means that all quantitative scientific models must ultimately be formulated as computational algorithms. But models can also be expressed as algorithms right from the start, and explored using computer simulation as the dominant tool.

Quantification of model complexity and randomness. Scientific models being algorithms, they can be analyzed using the tools of algorithmic information theory. Datasets can be analyzed similarly by considering them as the result of a computation. This makes it possible to define more rigorously the distinction between regularities explained by a model and random errors in observations.

Explicit treatment of uncertainties. Computational sampling from high-dimensional probability distributions has made the description of uncertainties in measurements and computational predictions practically possible.

Interactive data analysis and visualization. Most of the techniques used routinely today would be so cumbersome without electronic computers to render them practically useless.

There can be no doubt that these developments have vastly expanded our capacity for understanding natural phenomena and for improving our technology. However, they have also introduced attitudes and habits from the computing industry into scientific research which are not appropriate for science. Computing is an engineering domain whose priority is to produce tools for doing things. How the tools do their job is usually of little importance to their users, and often the subject of protected intellectual property. There is a clear division between manufacturers and users of software tools. Users do not have the competences required for understanding the software's source code, and often they do not even have access to it. They evaluate software purely by the services that it provides to them. This is in stark contrast to scientific research, where the methods and procedures used to obtain a result are at least as important as the result itself.

The massive use of computing has pushed a large part of scientific knowledge into the realm of software. For complex models, a description in terms of prose, mathematical equations, and tables would be very long and thus difficult to write down, read, or understand. A software implementation, in contrast, is guaranteed to be complete (otherwise it would not work), and can be used for simulation. For purely algorithmic models, a software implementation seems also more natural than a definition in plain language. But scientific software follows the logic of software as a tool. Today we find scientific communities divided into a small group of software developers and a large group of software users. The latter often do not know the exact models and methods that they are applying, because the software source code is too complicated for them to understand. Many scientific models thus have become black boxes.

Another habit of software development that is detrimental for science is the priority given to the continuous improvement of tools while neglecting the thorough documentation of all changes. Any change to a piece of software is likely to make it produce different results for identical inputs, even if the goal of the change is purely technical, such as making the program more efficient. This is particularly true for numerical computations (see also sections 3.6 and 5.2.6), where a change as minor as re-ordering terms in a sum can change the scientific interpretation of the results (examples are given in [17] and [18]). Program optimization almost always implies making or changing an approximation to a scientific model, but is almost never documented as such.

Finally, computers and software are generally known for their often unpredictable behavior, which is a consequence of the extreme complexity of modern software systems. I will discuss this aspect in detail in chapter 5. Scientists are victims of program crashes and other erroneous behaviors as much as other computer users, and yet most of them maintain the belief that the results obtained from scientific software should be considered correct unless there is good evidence to the contrary. This attitude is slowly changing [19], but techniques for evaluating the reliability of computational results are still missing.

2.6 Further reading

The role of models in science has been discussed extensively in the literature on the philosophy of science. A good introduction is Alan Chalmers' book *What is this thing called science?* [20]. For a concise and practical discussion of scientific models, written by a scientist for scientists, I recommend two articles by David Hestenes [21; 22].

Terence Tao's video lecture 'The Cosmic Distance Ladder' provides a lot of background information about the observation of celestial bodies and the mathematical interpretation of astronomical data.

Numerical analysis is a domain of research in its own right, and is backed up by a large body of literature. A good starting point for those mainly interested in applying tried and tested algorithms is *Numerical Recipes* by W H Press *et al* [23]. For a compact presentation of the fundamental ideas, see *A Student's Guide to Numerical Methods* by Ian Hutchinson [24]

Many books have also been written about complex systems over the last few decades. Two complementary introductions for a general scientific audience are John Holland's *Complexity* [25] and Robert B Laughlin's *A Different Universe* [26].

Climate research is an excellent illustration for the tendency that I outlined in section 2.2.5. Climate models are in fact non-trivial pieces of software. One of them, the Community Earth System Model, is Open Source software, allowing a detailed inspection by anyone.

The role of computation in modern biology is the topic of Hallam Stevens' *Life out of Sequence* [27], which describes how computers have changed not only how biologists work, but also what they consider worth studying.

In *The Rise of Computer-Aided Explanation* [28], Michael Nielsen gives examples for data-driven approaches to science and engineering problems. A more technical introduction to the emerging field of data science that manages to avoid the hype generally surrounding this topic is *Doing Data Science* by Cathy O'Neill and Rachel Schutt [29].

The November 2015 issue of *Computing in Science and Engineering* magazine has 'Computing and climate' as its theme. Several articles explain how traditional physical models are being complemented by generic empirical models that are adapted to observed data using machine learning techniques.

For an in-depth discussion of algorithmic information theory, including Kolmogorov complexity, logical depth, and their practical approximation in minimal description length approaches, a comprehensive source is *An Introduction to Kolmogorov Complexity and its Applications* by Ming Li and Paul Vitányi in reference [30]. For a nice illustration of the concepts in an application to music, see Christopher Ford's video presentation and its companion site.

References

[1] Copernicus N 1543 *De revolutionibus orbium cælestium* (Nuremberg: Johannes Petreius)
[2] Kepler J 1609 *Astronomia nova* (Heidelberg: Voegelin)
[3] Newton I 1687 *Philosophiæ Naturalis Principia Mathematica* (London: Royal Society)

[4] Pour-El M B and Ian Richards J 1989 *Computability in Analysis and Physics* (Berlin: Springer)

[5] Leibniz G W 1686 *Discours de métaphysique* http://fr.wikisource.org/wiki/Discours_de_m%C3%A9taphysique

[6] Ioannidis J P A 2005 Why most published research findings are false *PLoS Med.* **2** e124

[7] Jorgensen W L, Chandrasekhar J, Madura J D, Impey R W and Klein M L 1983 Comparison of simple potential functions for simulating liquid water *J. Chem. Phys.* **79** 926–35

[8] Pitt M A and Myung I J 2002 When a good fit can be bad *Trends Cogn. Sci.* **6** 421–5

[9] Pathway Logic http://pl.csl.sri.com/

[10] Kappa, a rule-based language for modeling protein interaction networks http://www.kappalanguage.org/

[11] Wolfram S 2002 *A New Kind of Science* (Champaign, IL: Wolfram Media)

[12] Aberth O 2001 *Computable Calculus* (New York: Academic)

[13] Goldstein H, Poole C P and Safko J L 2002 *Classical Mechanics* (Reading, MA: Addison Wesley)

[14] Džeroski S and Todorovski L (ed) 2007 *Computational Discovery of Scientific Knowledge* (Berlin: Springer)

[15] Lobo D and Levin M 2015 Inferring regulatory networks from experimental morphological phenotypes: A computational method reverse-engineers planarian regeneration *PLoS Comput. Biol.* **11** e1004295

[16] Mohr P J, Taylor B N and Newell D B 2012 Codata recommended values of the fundamental physical constants: 2010 *Rev. Mod. Phys.* **84** 1527–605

[17] Diethelm K 2012 The limits of reproducibility in numerical simulation *Comput. Sci. Eng.* **14** 64–72

[18] Gronenschild E H B M, Habets P, Jacobs H I L, Mengelers R, Rozendaal N, van Os J and Marcelis M 2012 The effects of freesurfer version, workstation type, and macintosh operating system version on anatomical volume and cortical thickness measurements *PLoS One* **7** e38234

[19] Merali Z 2010 *Computational science: …Error Nature* **467** 775–7

[20] Chalmers A F 2013 *What Is This Thing Called Science?* 4th edn (Indianapolis, IN: Hackett)

[21] Hestenes D 1992 Modeling games in the Newtonian world *Am. J. Phys.* **60** 732–48

[22] Hestenes D 2006 Notes for a modeling theory *Proc. of the 2006 GIREP Conf.: Modelling in Physics and Physics Education* ed E van den Berg, A Ellermeijer and O Slooten http://modeling.asu.edu/R&E/Notes_on_Modeling_Theory.pdf

[23] Press W H, Teukolsky S A, Vetterling W T and Flannery B P 2007 *Numerical Recipes: The Art of Scientific Computing* 3rd edn (Cambridge: Cambridge University Press)

[24] Hutchinson I H 2015 *A Student's Guide to Numerical Methods* student edn (Cambridge: Cambridge University Press)

[25] Holland J H 2014 *Complexity: A Very Short Introduction (Very Short Introductions)* 1st edn (Oxford: Oxford University Press)

[26] Laughlin R B 2006 *A Different Universe: Reinventing Physics from the Bottom Down* (New York: Basic Books)

[27] Stevens H 2013 *Life Out of Sequence: A Data-Driven History of Bioinformatics* 1st edn (Chicago, IL: University of Chicago Press)

[28] Nielsen M 2015 *The Rise of Computer-Aided Explanation* https://www.quantamagazine.org/the-rise-of-computer-aided-explanation-20150723/

[29] O'Neil C and Schutt R 2013 *Doing Data Science: Straight Talk from the Frontline* 1st edn (Sebastopol, CA: O'Reilly)

[30] Li M and Vitányi P 2008 *An Introduction to Kolmogorov Complexity and its Applications* (New York: Springer)

IOP Publishing

Computation in Science (Second Edition)
From concepts to practice
Konrad Hinsen

Chapter 3

Formalizing computation

As chapter 1 concluded, computation is the transformation of data, encoded as sequences of symbols, according to well-defined rules. When we perform computations by hand, using pencil and paper, we accept as 'data' anything that we can write down, and formulate our rules in terms of sentences in ordinary language. Often we invent shorthand notation or shortcuts in our rules as we proceed in our work, guided by the meaning of what we are computing. Before sharing our computations with others, we therefore often clean them up and introduce a more systematic notation. Before publishing them in a scientific journal, we usually ask someone else to verify our work, both to find and correct mistakes and to make sure that all notation has been explained well enough for readers to be able to follow our steps.

If we want to delegate a computational task to a machine, we have to introduce more rigor and precision. A machine does not understand the meaning of our computations. It cannot guess definitions or rules that may seem obvious to us from the context. It will not watch out for nonsense computations either. There is a long way to go from the informal rules we learn in school for performing arithmetic on decimal numbers with pencil and paper to a program instructing a computer to perform the corresponding state transitions in its memory. It is helpful to establish some middle ground, by constructing formal models of computation.

There are many formal models of computation, which were designed for very different purposes. One such purpose is writing programs for computing machines. Programming languages, or at least *some* programming languages, form the most pragmatic end of the spectrum of formal models of computation. As we will see in chapter 4, many popular programming languages do not fully qualify because their specification is incomplete or ambiguous. In this chapter, we will look at a few formal models of computation developed for the theoretical analysis of computation. Some of these models were constructed in order to explore the nature of computation itself, whereas others were designed to help in applying computation for solving real-world problems. The number of different models is enormous, and

I will not even try to provide an exhaustive overview. Instead, I will concentrate on a few models that are useful for computation in science or for understanding how computation works in general.

3.1 From manual computation to rewriting rules

Our first formal model of computation is one that is very close to the way we manipulate mathematical formulas in manual computation. Let us start with a simple example. To compute the derivative

$$\frac{d}{dx}(\sin x)^2, \tag{3.1}$$

we use two elementary differentiation rules,

$$\frac{d}{dx}\sin x = \cos x \tag{3.2}$$

$$\frac{d}{dx}x^n = nx^{n-1}, \tag{3.3}$$

plus the chain rule

$$\frac{d}{dx}f(g(x)) = f'(g(x)) \cdot g'(x), \tag{3.4}$$

where $f'(x) = \frac{d}{dx}f(x)$. The detailed steps are:

$$\frac{d}{dx}(\sin x)^2$$
$$= \frac{d}{dx}f(g(x)) \text{ with } f(y) = y^2, \quad g(x) = \sin x$$
$$= f'(g(x)) \cdot g'(x) \text{ with } f'(y) = 2y, \quad g'(x) = \cos x$$
$$= 2 \cdot \sin x \cdot \cos x$$

There are more rules for differentiation, of course, in particular for many more elementary functions. From the complete set of rules, we pick those that match the problem at hand. This rather mechanical application of rules to mathematical expressions satisfies all the conditions for being a computation. It is, in fact, a kind of computation handled routinely by computer algebra systems.

As written above, the problem statement and the rules make sense to someone who has taken a course in calculus. If we want a computer to do the work for us, we have to make all the implicit context of calculus explicit, and cast the differentiation task into a fixed set of rules that can be applied mechanically to any expression, without the need to understand their meaning.

As a first step, we define a formal notation for mathematical expressions. We define a *term* to be an *operator* followed by any number of *arguments* written in parentheses, e.g. op(arg_1, arg_2, ... arg_N). The operator is just a name, made up of arbitrary characters. For simplicity, we will allow only the lower-case characters a to z. Each argument is again an arbitrary term. If the number of arguments is zero, we do not write the parentheses for simplicity. With these rules, x is a term: a single zero-argument operator, and sin(x) is also a term: the one-argument operator sin whose argument is the term x. But x^2 is not a term, nor is ab (multiplication). We can easily rewrite such expressions to fit into our schema: x^2 becomes power(x, 2) and ab becomes mult(a, b). Unfortunately, power(x, 2) is still not a term because 2 is not a term. It is possible but cumbersome to express integers as terms[1], so we will follow the approach taken by practical computation systems based on term algebras and accept integers as 'special' terms.

Our definition for terms is very general at this stage. Before doing any useful computation with terms, we need to impose additional constraints on what terms we consider acceptable. In particular, we provide an explicit list of allowed operators, and specify for each operator how many arguments it requires. Such a specification defines a *term algebra*. For our differentiation problem, we need the zero-argument operator x, the one-argument operators sin and cos, and the two-argument operators power and diff, with the latter being introduced for differentiation. We can then write equation (3.1) as

```
diff(power(sin(x), 2), x).
```

We introduce the notation $\mathbb{T}$ for the set of all valid terms in our term algebra.

Next, we must formalize our rules for differentiation to *term rewriting rules*:

$(a)\,\forall\;\;X \in \mathbb{T},\;\;V \in \mathbb{V}$:
```
diff(sin(X), V) → mult(cos(X), diff(X, V))
```
$(b)\,\forall\;\;X \in \mathbb{T},\;\;V \in \mathbb{V},\;\;N \in \mathbb{Z}$:
```
diff(power(X, N), V) → mult(mult(N, power(X, N−1)),
                           diff(X, V))
```

The symbol $\forall$ means 'for all', i.e. $\forall X \in \mathbb{T}$ means 'for all X that are members of the set $\mathbb{T}$'. In addition to the set $\mathbb{T}$ of all valid terms, we have used the set $\mathbb{Z}$ of all integers and the set $\mathbb{V}$ of all independent variables. The latter is a subset of $\mathbb{T}$, because all independent variables are also valid terms In our example, $\mathbb{V}$ contains only one element, the term x.

Each rule consists of three parts. On the left-hand side of the arrow, a *pattern* defines the structure of the terms to which the rule can be applied. A pattern is a term containing placeholders[2] that can stand for any term. In the above example, all

---

[1] The basic idea is to have a zero-argument operator zero and two one-argument operators increment and decrement, which are composed to make up arbitrary numbers, i.e. increment(increment(increment (zero))) for the number 3.
[2] Placeholders are usually called *variables* in the literature on term rewriting, but I already use that word for differentiation variables in this section.

upper-case names are placeholders. The exact kind of term that each placeholder can stand for is defined in the conditions given on the first line of each rule.

If we apply these three rules repeatedly to the initial term `diff(power(sin (x), 2), x)` and its subterms, we ultimately obtain a term in which no rule can be applied any more, because no rule's left-hand side matches the term or its subterms Such a term is called a *normal form*. For our example it is `mult(2, mult(cos (x), mult(diff(x, x), power(sin(x), 1))))`. This is indeed the right result for our differentiation problem, but it would benefit from some simplifications. Ideally, we want to obtain the form `mult(2, mult(cos(x), sin(x)))`. This requires three more rules:

$(c)\ \forall$ $V \in \mathbb{V}$: `diff(V, V)` $\rightarrow 1$

$(d)\ \forall$ $X \in \mathbb{T}$: `power(X, 1)` $\rightarrow X$

$(e)\ \forall$ $X \in$ `:mult(1, X)` $\rightarrow X$

Rule (c) says that $dx/dx = 1$, rule (d) says that $x^1 = x$, and rule (e) says that $1 \cdot x = x$.

Comparing the term rewriting rules (a) to (e) with the three informal rules in equations (3.2)–(3.4), we note a few important differences. First of all, the term rewriting rules (c)–(e) have no equivalent in the informal rule set. They are part of the *tacit knowledge* of the field. Everyone would take it for granted that a person with even minimal knowledge of algebra and calculus would apply these simplifications automatically. Second, the chain rule has been integrated with the elementary differentiation rules in (a) and (b). This is necessary because no valid term in our system corresponds to an unapplied function such as sin. Since placeholders can only stand for terms, there is no way to have a placeholder for 'any function f of one variable'.

It is worth noting that the rules (a)–(e) express mathematical identities, i.e. the terms on the left-hand side and on the right-hand side of each rule are mathematically equal for all allowed values of the placeholders. A rule can be seen as a mathematical equation with an additional direction in which it is applied. However, the interpretation of rules as mathematical equations is part of the *semantics* of our formalism, not of its definition. It is perfectly possible to write mathematically incorrect rules, such as `diff(sin(X), V)` $\rightarrow$ `cos(X)`, i.e. forgetting the chain rule. From the point of view of the computational model, such a rule is perfectly valid, although in view of the intended mathematical interpretation it is erroneous.

I have not been very precise about how rules are applied to terms in the computation process. It is possible that at some step in the process, several rules can be applied. When that happens, which rule should be chosen? The answer is that for the rules (a)–(e) given above, it does not matter: the final result will always be the same, because this particular set of rules is *confluent*. In general, the result can depend on the order of application of rules, and therefore it is necessary to specify a rule application strategy in order to define a computation completely. One simple strategy is to apply the rules in order, i.e. first apply rule (a) as often as possible, and move on to rule (b) afterwards.

Another aspect that requires more attention is the termination of the term rewriting process. It is easy to come up with a rule that will cause infinite computation, for example the rule

$$\forall \quad X \in \mathbb{T}: f(X) \rightarrow f(f(X))$$

We will see later that any sufficiently powerful formal model of computation allows non-terminating computations. For term rewriting systems, certain sets of rules can be shown to terminate, but in general neither termination nor non-termination can be proven.

A more practical question is how one can be sure that a given term algebra with its associated rewrite rules is sufficient to perform the computation it was designed for. We have seen above that the rules (a) and (b) alone were not sufficient for our goals, which is why we added rules (c)–(e). This is a variant of the general question in computing of how to ensure that a computer program does what it is supposed to do. While certain properties can be proven mathematically, the intention behind a computation escapes formalization and is thus out of the reach of mathematical proofs. Like any piece of software, a term rewriting system must be tested (see section 5.2) to verify that it does what its author claims it does.

There are programming languages based on term rewriting, which allow a rather direct implementation of the computations discussed in this section. An implementation of the differentiation problem in a language called Maude [1] is available from the companion web site to this book for further exploration.

The above example illustrates the transition from informally specified rules for manipulating mathematical expressions to a formal model for computation, term rewriting. In scientific computing, the most popular application of term rewriting is computer algebra systems, which perform tasks that are similar to our example. In software engineering, term rewriting is used in *specification languages*, which are used to define *what* a program is supposed to compute without going into the details of *how* it should do so. In this case, term rewriting is used as a computational model because its proximity to mathematical equations facilitates the application of formal proofs of correctness.

3.2 From computing machines to automata theory

Term rewriting systems are a formal model of computation that is close to the mathematical end of the bridge we want to construct towards the bit-level operations in a digital computer. Now we will look at the other end of this bridge, where we find formal models that resemble the operation of a digital computer, but represent the data being worked on in a more convenient form than sequences of bits. Moreover, these models do not try to describe all aspects of a real computer, for example its speed or energy consumption. This approach to the theory of computation is known as *automata theory*.

The most famous and arguably most important automaton model of computation is the *Turing machine*, which was invented in 1936 by Alan Turing, one of the pioneers of the theory of computation, who called it simply an 'automatic machine' [2].

Turing's ideas heavily influenced the design of electronic digital computers, which was starting around the same time. The Turing machine is an abstract mathematical construct, but it can be implemented as a physical device, as has been demonstrated by two teams [3, 4] who built Lego versions to celebrate Alan Turing's 100th birthday in 2012.

A Turing machine consists of
- an internal state, which can take any value from a fixed finite set;
- an infinite tape divided into squares, each of which can be blank or contain a single symbol from a fixed finite alphabet;
- a read/write head that is at any time positioned on one square of the tape;
- a finite instruction table that defines the machine's operation.

The machine proceeds in discrete steps. At each step, it looks up an instruction from its instruction table. Each entry in this table has five elements. The first two elements are the current internal state and the symbol on the tape at the position of the head. These two elements determine if a specific entry can be applied at a given step in the machine's operation, i.e. they serve the same purpose as the pattern in a term rewriting rule. The remaining three elements specify the three actions taken by the machine:
- First, write a symbol to the current tape position. Erasing a square is a special case of writing a symbol.
- Second, move the head along the tape by a distance of −1, 0, or 1.
- Third, change the internal state to a specified new value.

A Turing machine starts in a special 'initial' state with a tape that is blank except for the squares that contain the input to its computation. It stops when it cannot apply any of the instructions in its table. The output of the computation is the contents of the tape at that moment. A Turing machine may never stop for certain input tapes, but rather get stuck in an endless loop. In that case, it produces no output and does no useful work.

A rough analogy with a modern digital computer can be established by identifying the tape with the working memory plus external storage, the internal state with the processor registers, and the instruction table with the processor's instruction set. The most important fundamental difference between a Turing machine and a real computer is the Turing machine's infinite tape, compared to the necessarily finite memory of any physical machine. The tape is the only unlimited resource of a Turing machine. Everything else (the internal state, the alphabet of the tape, the instruction table) has a finite size.

In its original form, the Turing machine has a fixed 'program' given by its instruction table. This program reads input from the tape and writes output back to the tape. However, as Turing himself already noticed, it is possible to construct a 'universal' Turing machine that can emulate the behavior of any other Turing machine by reading that machine's instruction table from the tape. This observation turns out to be one of the most important discoveries about computation. It is what permits the construction of a single computing machine capable of performing any computation, given the right 'software'. Nearly all of today's computers work according to this principle.

Beyond the practical aspect of making universal computing machines possible, Turing's discovery also establishes that there is no fundamental distinction between a 'program' and the 'data' it works on. Both are sequences of symbols on the tape of a universal Turing machine. The whole tape can be considered the 'input data' of that machine, the program being defined by the instruction table. Inversely, the whole tape can be considered a program not requiring any further input. Finally, any sequence of symbols on the tape can be fed to a universal Turing machine as a program, even though in most cases this does not lead to any useful result. In our day-to-day computational work, we maintain the distinction between programs and data mainly because they tend to come from different sources and are managed in different ways. However, any attempt to formalize this distinction is bound to fail. Programs are nothing but data being interpreted as instructions.

3.3 Computability

The goal that Turing pursued with his theoretical machine was to explore which mathematical functions or properties can in principle be computed in a mechanical fashion. He did this in the context of an important mathematical question of his time: is it possible to decide mechanically, by mindlessly manipulating symbols without any attention to their meaning, if a given mathematical statement follows from a given set of axioms? In other words, can mathematics be reduced to axioms plus computation? This was the ambitious goal formulated by David Hilbert in 1928, known as the 'Entscheidungsproblem' (German for 'decision problem'), and Turing's work was one of the decisive contributions to proving this goal impossible to achieve.

Much of the mathematical research around this subject concentrated on theorems about numbers, which is why Turing's focus was the set of 'computable numbers'. He defined them as 'the real numbers whose expressions as a decimal are calculable by finite means'. The qualification 'by finite means' is particularly important in Turing's definition of computability. If we want to use a computing machine as a tool to get some work done, we are not interested in exploring unrealistic limits such as machines of infinite size or energy consumption, or computations of infinite duration.

The use of an infinite tape in Turing's machine may seem like a contradiction at first sight. However, any finite computation uses only a finite part of the tape. The machine's read–write head can move by at most one square per computational step, and therefore an N-step computation cannot use more than N squares. The requirement of an infinite tape merely avoids imposing an arbitrary limit on the size of the computational problems that a Turing machine can handle. The same can be said of the duration of a computation. It is required to be finite, as otherwise there would be no result, but there is no upper bound on the number of steps imposed by the construction of Turing's machine. We can make the same observation about the term rewriting approach from section 3.1. Both the length of a term and the number of rule applications are unrestricted in principle, but both must remain finite in any operation that counts as a computation.

In general it is difficult to find out if a number or function defined by some statement or formula is computable or not. A proof of computability is usually constructive, i.e. it provides an algorithm that performs the computation. Proofs of non-computability often proceed by contradiction. The most famous non-computable problem is known as the *halting problem*. As I mentioned earlier, a Turing machine either stops with its output on the tape, or it continues to compute indefinitely. Is it possible to decide by computation if a universal Turing machine will stop for a given input tape, containing its program and input data? The answer is no. For a *specific* input tape, it may well be possible to decide if the machine's operation comes to an end, but there is no algorithm that can reach this conclusion for an *arbitrary* input tape. Note that simply executing the program is not an option. If at some point it stops, the answer is obvious, but how long should one wait before concluding that it will never stop?

Many characteristics of Turing's machine are chosen in an arbitrary fashion, which raises the question of whether some other machine could possibly compute a wider range of numbers, and thus lead to a more general definition of computability. To this day, nobody has succeeded in constructing such a more powerful machine. Moreover, other mathematicians working on the question of computability have proposed very different formal models, which were shown to be equivalent to Turing machines in the sense that each of these formal models can emulate any other one. The best known model of this kind is Alonzo Church's λ-calculus [5], which was published around the same time as Turing's work. It is based on a formal definition of so-called λ-terms and associated rules that define how λ-terms can be transformed to equivalent λ-terms.

The statement that the most powerful models of computation are those that are equivalent to Turing machines or λ-calculus is known as the Church–Turing thesis. It is impossible to prove correct, but it could be proven wrong by the construction of a counterexample, i.e. more powerful model of computation. A model of computation that is equivalent to a Turing machine is called *Turing-complete*. The term-rewriting model illustrated in section 3.1 is such a Turing-complete model.

3.4 Restricted models of computation

Whereas no one has succeeded to this day in constructing a model of computation that is more powerful than a Turing machine, there are a number of models that are intentionally *less* powerful, i.e. they are not Turing-complete. There are two reasons for considering such restricted models. First, they can describe the behavior of real physical systems, whose computational aspects one wishes to study theoretically. Second, they can be of use in software engineering because they offer stronger guarantees than Turing-complete models. For example, constraints added to prevent mistakes (such as accidental infinite loops) can make a model practically more useful even though they remove Turing-completeness. I will come back to this in section 4.2.1.

A well-studied restricted model of computation is the *finite state machine*, which differs from a Turing machine in that the head can move only in one direction along the tape. This may seem like a small difference, but it means that the tape cannot be used for storing intermediate results in a computation, because the machine cannot read back a symbol that it has written earlier. As the computation proceeds, input symbols are read from the tape and are replaced by output symbols. The result of the computation consists of the output symbols and the final state of the machine. Finite state machines are of interest because they describe the behavior of many physical systems, both natural and man-made. The classical textbook example is a vending machine, whose input sequence consists of user actions (push a button, insert a coin) and whose output sequence is the machine's actions: deliver a product, display message, etc. An example for a natural system that can be described approximately by a finite-state machine is a network of neurons [6]. Unlike a Turing machine, a finite-state machine can never get stuck in an endless loop, which is a useful feature in machine learning (see section 4.2.2), where artificial neural networks are very popular.

Another class of models of computation that has been widely studied because it describes aspects of physical systems is the class of cellular automata, which I have already mentioned in section 2.2.5. Strictly speaking, I should not mention them under the heading of 'restricted models', because some cellular automata can be shown to be Turing-complete. However, this is usually an accidental byproduct rather than a design goal. A cellular automaton consists of cells arranged on a grid. This grid can have any dimension, though 1, 2, and 3 dimensions are the most common. Each cell has a state that is a value from a fixed and finite set. Usually this set is very small, having two or three elements. Finally, the definition of a cellular automaton provides a finite set of transition rules that determine how the state of all cells changes from one computational step to the next.

3.5 Computational complexity

Computability guarantees that a result can be computed using finite resources in finite time, but the resources or time required may still be prohibitively large. Not only large compared to the computational power available to a researcher at any given time, but also large compared to the resources of the Universe. A computation that takes a year today may well become doable in a minute a few years from now, due to improvements in computing technology. But a computation whose duration exceeds the age of the Universe is likely to remain out of reach forever. Similar considerations apply to memory usage. A computation that requires the storage of more bits than there are atoms in the solar system can be considered impossible for all practical purposes.

Most computational tasks in science can be characterized by some number N that describes the amount of data that must be processed. This N can be the number of atoms in a simulation of a liquid, for example, or the number of samples in an experimental dataset. The most precise definition of N is the number of bits required to store the information to be processed. The time and memory required for performing a computation grow as functions of N. The details of these functions depend on the hardware and software available for the task, but it is nevertheless possible to deduce some important properties from a theoretical analysis of the algorithms that are applied. Of particular interest is the asymptotic behavior for large N, which is called the *computational complexity* of an algorithm. There are several different measures of computational complexity, depending on the feature of interest: time or memory, worst-case or average behavior, etc.

The complexity of an algorithm is usually given as $O(f(N))$, with $f(N)$ a simple function such as N^2 or e^N. This notation means that the fastest-growing term is proportional to $f(N)$. Constant prefactors and terms that grow more slowly are considered irrelevant. Of course they may well be relevant in practice, as a constant factor of 1000 often makes the difference between a doable and an impossible computation. However, the goal of computational complexity theory is not the study of what can reasonably be computed at a given moment, but the distinction between fundamentally tractable and intractable problems. With this goal in mind, algorithms are lumped into even more coarse-grained *complexity classes*. An important complexity class is P, the class of algorithms whose execution time grows no faster than some polynomial in N. This class contains all algorithms with $O(N^p)$ for some p, but also those for which a polynomial function is an upper bound, e.g. $O(N \log N)$. Other important complexity classes are EXP, which includes algorithms whose time is exponential in a polynomial of N, and PSPACE, which contains all algorithms whose memory requirements are polynomial in N. These classes have convenient properties for mathematical reasoning. For example, combining two algorithms from class P yields another algorithm in class P. Many general properties can be proven about these classes. For example, it can be shown that class P is a subset of class PSPACE, i.e. an algorithm with polynomial run time also has memory requirements bounded by a polynomial function.

The practical implications of these complexity classes are illustrated by figure 3.1, which was inspired by figure 2.5 of [7]. It shows the run time of algorithms in classes P (green) and EXP (red) as a function of N, assuming a run time of 1 ms for $N = 1$. While even members of class P can reach prohibitive run times, those in class EXP get there much earlier. Such algorithms can be used in practice only for very small N. A well-known example for an exponential-time algorithm in computational science is the simulation of quantum-mechanical systems [8]. A full description of the quantum state of N spins (e.g. N electrons) requires 2^N complex numbers, and simulating its time evolution is an $O(2^N)$ algorithm. This problem has motivated the development of quantum computation. Aside from such rare exceptions, all algorithms used in computational science are in class P for the simple reason that otherwise they would not be useful in practice.

It is not immediately obvious that computational complexity is practically relevant for designing algorithms and software. An algorithm that is $O(N^p)$ for some large p may well be as intractable as one that is $O(e^N)$ for all practical purposes. Even a large prefactor can be a significant practical issue. Complexity classes are thus not the last word on the resource requirements of algorithms. However, there are empirical arguments supporting their study. For example, it

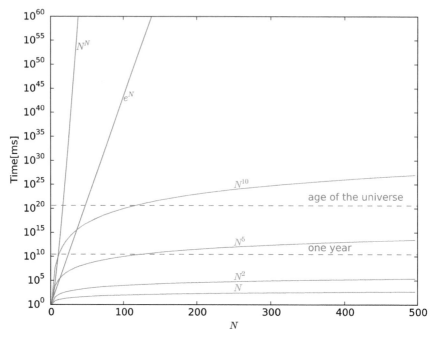

Figure 3.1. The time required for a computation of size N assuming that for $N = 1$ the time is 1 ms. The green curves show polynomial growth, the red curve exponential behavior.

turns out that the vast majority of algorithms that solve practically relevant problems either have small p or are not in class P at all. Moreover, determining an algorithm's complexity usually contributes to a better understanding of the algorithm, and thus shows where there is potential for improvement.

The most famous open question in complexity theory is whether class P is equal to class NP. Class NP contains search problems of the type 'is there any solution x such that condition $p(x)$ is true'. More precisely, class NP contains all problems of this type whose $p(x)$ can be computed in polynomial time, N being a measure of the size of x. In other words, checking the validity of a candidate solution is a class P problem. Such problems are of enormous practical importance. A popular example is a variant of the *travelling salesman problem*: Given N cities on a map, check if there is a closed loop itinerary that passes through each city exactly once, and whose length is at most L. Computing the length of a candidate itinerary is $O(N^1)$ and thus in class P, but the most efficient known algorithms for finding an itinerary of length L or less are $O(e^N)$. Most researchers suspect that no solution in P exists, meaning that P $\neq$ NP, but no proof of this suspicion has been found to this day.

Problems of class NP are those that we think of as requiring creativity to solve, because a brute-force trial-and-error approach is much too inefficient. An example from science is finding a mathematical model for a set of observations that is shorter than the list of observations itself (see section 2.2.4). If we 'dream up' a candidate solution, which is where creativity comes in, it is easy to check whether it is a good one[3]. On the other hand, an exhaustive search through the set of all possible mathematical models is hopeless. If P = NP, finding such a model would be a tractable computation, a discovery that would probably lead to a major revolution in science.

3.6 Computing with numbers

Numbers are of prime importance in computational science, because most scientific models are quantitative. In sections 1.1.2 and 2.2.5, I have explained why it is impossible to compute with real numbers, and why this is a fundamental problem wherever computation needs to be applied to geometry. The formal models of computation of sections 3.1 and 3.2 cannot accommodate numbers unless they are represented by finite sequences of symbols. In the following, I will take a closer look at three subsets of the real numbers that can and have been used in for numerical computations: the set of floating-point numbers, the set of rational numbers, and the set of computable numbers. As we will see, each of them has its particular advantages and difficulties.

3.6.1 Floating-point numbers

The floating-point numbers are actually a family of sets. A specific set of floating-point numbers is defined by a *floating-point format*, of which the most widely used ones are the single-precision and double-precision binary floating-point formats defined by IEEE standard 754. Floating-point numbers are constructed with the goal that any real number inside a reasonably large interval can be approximated by a floating-point number in such a way that the relative error of the approximation is bounded. This is achieved by using an exponential representation of the form $s \cdot m \cdot b^e$, where the sign s is -1 or 1, the mantissa m is a natural number, the basis b is a natural number, and the exponent e is an integer. Most floating-point formats use $b = 2$ for a convenient representation in terms of bit sequences, but $b = 10$ is sometimes used for human convenience—this is how we compute with pencil and paper, after all. Every number written in this form is a rational number, but not all rational numbers can be expressed in this way. A simple counterexample for $b = 10$ is 1/3, whose decimal representation is the infinite stream of digits 0.333.... The ranges of m and e are further restrained in order to make s, m, and e fit into a fixed number of bits. The set of floating-point numbers is therefore finite, with a smallest and a largest element, and a gap between any two neighboring values. This is illustrated in figure 3.2, which shows the 79 numerical values allowed by a binary ($b = 2$) floating-point format with an unusually small size: four bits for the mantissa, and exponents between -4 and 2. Most floating-point formats, including those

---

[3] Unless, of course, the candidate model contains an algorithm that is not in complexity class P—but such models are not very useful anyway.

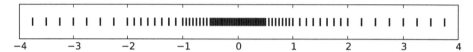

Figure 3.2. The 79 possible values in a floating-point format with a four-bit mantissa and an exponent range from −4 to 2.

defined by IEEE standard 754, define some bit patterns in a special way, to represent infinities and the results of invalid operations, but I will not discuss them here.

A major inconvenience of floating-point numbers is that the sum or product of two floating-point numbers can in general not be written as a floating-point number in the same format as its inputs. As an example, consider a decimal ($b = 10$) floating-point format with a one-digit mantissa. The values $a = 0.4$ and $b = 0.02$ can be represented in this format, but their sum $a + b = 0.42$ cannot—it would require a two-digit mantissa. Arithmetic operations are therefore defined by adding a *rounding step*: the floating-point sum of two numbers is the floating-point number closest to their exact sum within the given format. In the example I used above, the sum of a and b thus becomes $a \oplus b = 0.4$, i.e. it is identical to a! Note that I use $\oplus$ for floating-point addition to distinguish it clearly from the + for standard addition.

Due to the added rounding step, computations on floating-point numbers differ in important respects from arithmetic on integers, rational numbers, or real numbers, which we are all familiar with from our school days. The most important property that is lost by the introduction of rounding is the associativity of sums and products: in floating-point arithmetic, $(a \oplus b) \oplus c \neq a \oplus (b \oplus c)$. In the above example, complemented by introducing $c = 0.04$, we have $(a \oplus b) \oplus c = (0.4 \oplus 0.02) \oplus 0.04 = 0.4 \oplus 0.04 = 0.4$ and $a \oplus (b \oplus c) = 0.4 \oplus (0.02 \oplus 0.04) = 0.4 \oplus 0.06 = 0.5$. In the first sum, we twice add a small number to a big number, losing the small number completely in the rounding step. In the second sum, the two small numbers are added first, yielding a big enough value to make a difference when added to the big number. The exact sum of the three numbers is 0.46, and the nearest floating-point value in our format is 0.5, meaning that the second summation order gives a more accurate result. In general, numbers of equal sign should be added from smallest to largest. This rule and others like it can be found in the literature. They are rarely applied in practice, sometimes out of ignorance and sometimes because of the added cost—sorting a list of numbers before summing them makes the computation of the sum much more expensive. A more fundamental problem is that decades of assuming associativity for the addition of numbers since our math courses in school have created habits that make it very difficult to drop this assumption when writing computer programs. Most scientists quickly write a program for 'summing N numbers' without even realizing that the very definition of the task has become ambiguous with floating-point arithmetic. This ambiguity can be important enough to change the conclusions made on the basis of a computation (see [9] for an example).

The implicit rounding step in every floating-point operation is also the reason for the first rule that everyone learns about floating-point numbers: never test two floating-point values for equality. This is not a hard rule without exceptions, as there are a few situations where equality tests make sense. But in general, equality conditions between computed values are broken by the loss of precision due to rounding. Unfortunately, the simple rule that everyone learns only says what one should *not* do. But what to do instead? The usual answer is to test for approximate equality, i.e. replace a test for $a = b$ by a test for $\text{abs}(a - b) < \epsilon$. This raises the question of what ϵ should be, i.e. how to decide if an approximate rounded result is 'good enough'. Unfortunately, there is no universal answer to this question. The choice of ϵ depends both on the floating-point format and on the computation that is being performed.

The major advantage of rounding after every operation is that all numerical computations happen within a finite set of numbers, whose binary representation has a fixed size. It is therefore possible to anticipate both the storage required for the result of an arbitrary computation and its duration, without knowing anything about the values that are processed. We will see later that rational numbers and computable numbers do not have this property. This is why floating-point numbers are by far the most widely used number representation in scientific computing.

Floating-point arithmetic has the reputation of being somehow imprecise and unpredictable. This reputation has its origins in the many different floating-point conventions that were in use in the early days of electronic computers. Both the storage formats and the exact definition of arithmetic operations varied widely between computer systems. The same program (in terms of, say, Fortran source code) would thus produce different results on different computers. The IEEE 754 standard, published in 1985, has improved the situation significantly. However, processor architectures and programming languages that predate IEEE 754 are still in widespread use. Writing a program using IEEE 754 floating-point operations without any deviation from the norm remains a major challenge. The remaining aura of fuzziness that surrounds floating-point numbers is exploited by compiler writers, who do not hesitate to re-arrange floating-point operations during code optimization even if this changes the results. They argue that programmers cannot expect a well-defined result anyway, given today's incomplete support for IEEE 754 in programming languages. They should thus happily accept some more variability in return for faster execution. Unfortunately, this attitude of compiler writers makes testing numerical software very difficult, a point I will come back to in section 5.2.

3.6.2 Rational numbers

Rational numbers can be represented exactly in a computer, most simply as a pair of two integers, the numerator and the denominator. In order to simplify operations, it is useful to impose a normalized representation in which the denominator is always positive, and the greatest common divisor of numerator and denominator is 1. Basic arithmetic on rational numbers can be performed exactly, as long as the computer has sufficient memory space to store the results.

Rational number arithmetic becomes problematic when fractional powers (e.g. square roots) or transcendental functions (e.g. logarithms) must be computed. The square root of a rational number is in general not a rational number, nor is its sine or logarithm. All of these values can be approximated to any desired precision by a rational number, but in practice the choice of this precision is not obvious. This is one of the reasons why rational arithmetic is rarely used in scientific computing. With floating-point numbers, which form a finite set, approximations are much more straightforward to perform, because the choice of precision has been made beforehand.

A less obvious but even more important argument against the use of rational arithmetic is its computational complexity. As more and more rational numbers are combined in the course of a lengthy computation, both numerators and denominators tend to grow in size. As an illustration, consider the sum 1/3 + 2/7, yielding 13/21. We can store 1/3 using 1 + 2 = 3 bits,[4] and 2/7 using 2 + 3 = 5 bits, but for storing the sum 13/21, we need 4 + 5 = 9 bits. This is the same phenomenon that we have seen in the floating-point example above, where the exact sum of 0.4 and 0.02 requires more storage space (a larger floating-point format) than either of its inputs. In lengthy iterative computations, such as the simulation of the solar system described in section 2.1.2, the size of the number representations tends to grow at every step, making rational arithmetic impractical for such applications.

Rational and floating-point arithmetic make different trade-offs: rational arithmetic maintains the highest possible precision, accepting increasing memory use and processor time, whereas floating-point arithmetic limits the use of computational resources by sacrificing precision.

3.6.3 Computable numbers

As I have explained in section 1.1.2, it is not possible to compute with real numbers, because a single real number contains an infinite amount of information. However, it is possible to compute with a subset of the real numbers that is larger than the rational numbers. Consider for example the square root of two, whose non-rational nature was already known to Greek mathematicians more than 2000 years ago. We thus cannot write it as the quotient of two integers. But we *can* write a computer program that produces a rational approximation to any precision we like. For illustration, here is such a program written in the Python language:

```
from fractions import Fraction

def square_root(x, eps):

    def iterate(a, b):
        mean = (a + b) / 2
        if abs(a-b) < eps:
```

---

[4] In addition to the bits for storing the numerators and denominators, we need to store information about how many bits we actually use, but I will ignore this for the sake of simplifying the discussion.

```
            return mean
        else:
            return iterate(mean, x/mean)

    return iterate(1, x)

print(square_root(Fraction(2, 1), Fraction(1, 100)))
```

This algorithm for computing square roots was first described in the 1st century by Hero of Alexandria. The function `square_root` takes a rational number x and another rational number ϵ indicating the desired precision, and returns a rational number s with the property abs$(s - \sqrt{x}) < \epsilon$. Note that rational numbers are called `Fraction` in Python and are implemented in the module `fractions`, i.e. they are not part of the basic Python language.

The computer program shown above allows us to find out everything we can ever know about the value of a square root. So why not use this program as a representation of the square root of 2? All we need for computing with numbers is a representation in terms of finite sequences of symbols. A computer program satisfies this criterion very well.

The same approach can be used for any other number for which we can compute a rational approximation to any desired precision. The set of all numbers for which this can be done is called the *computable numbers*, and was the subject of Turing's famous 1936 publication that introduced the Turing machine (see section 3.2). As Turing showed, the computable numbers contain the rational numbers (trivially), the algebraic numbers (the roots of all polynomials with integer coefficients), and many other numbers of practical interest, including π and e. Many functions of computable numbers can also be shown to be computable, e.g. the sine or the logarithm. Geometry, the field for which real numbers were invented, can thus be treated by computable numbers as well. However, most real numbers are not computable, which can be seen using the same reasoning that I have used in section 1.1.2: computer programs can be represented as sequences of symbols, and therefore form a countably infinite set, just like the integers and the rational numbers. Since the set of real numbers is not countable, most real numbers cannot be represented by a computer program.

There are some interesting parallels between computable numbers and physical measurements, which are related to the fact that both represent a numerical value with finite precision. Strict equality is undecidable for both computable numbers and measurements, meaning that comparisons can be made only up to the available precision. For computable numbers, this precision can be made arbitrarily small, but not zero. Moreover, computable functions of computable numbers are always continuous, because discontinuities can only be described in the unattainable limit of infinite precision. This is analogous to the effect of finite instrument resolution on experimental curves, e.g. in spectroscopy.

Computable numbers remove one of the disadvantages of rational arithmetic: most if not all numbers of interest in scientific computing can be represented exactly, without any need for arbitrary choices of precision. However, the other disadvantage of rational arithmetic, the ever-increasing resource requirements, becomes an even more serious problem. As an illustration, consider the addition of two computable numbers. Assume that a and b are computable numbers, represented by functions $a(\epsilon)$ and $b(\epsilon)$ that take a rational precision argument ϵ and return a corresponding rational approximation. Then their sum s is a computable number represented by the function $s(\epsilon) = a(\epsilon/2) + b(\epsilon/2)$. Note that a and b must be computed to twice the precision requested for s, because in the worst case, the approximations to both a and b are off by $\epsilon/2$. It is this necessity to always take into account the worst case that makes the precision increase rapidly as more and more arithmetic operations are combined.

3.7 Further reading

There are a large number of textbooks on the theory of computation. A book that stands out by its clarity of presentation is *The Nature of Computation* by Moore and Mertens [7], which places a strong emphasis on computational complexity. Automata theory is not treated in this book, but is discussed in most other textbooks, for example in the *Introduction to Automata Theory, Languages, and Computation* by Hopcroft, Motwani, and Ullman [10]. Another remarkable book on theoretical computer science is Tom Stuart's *Understanding Computation* [11], which explains the theoretical concepts by working Ruby programs—a nice illustration of how computation helps understanding (section 1.2), applied to computation itself. Douglas Hofstadter's Pulitzer-prize winning *Gödel, Escher, Bach* [12] discusses many aspects of the theory of computation in the wider context of recursion and self-reference in the human mind.

The book *Term Rewriting and All That* by F Baader and T Nipkow [13] provides a good and very complete introduction to term rewriting techniques. The ultimate reference for complexity classes is the *Complexity Zoo* web site [14].

For a comprehensive treatment of floating-point arithmetic, see the *Handbook of Floating-Point Arithmetic* by J-M Muller *et al* [15]. A more compact overview is given in the first chapter of Warwick Tucker's *Validated Numerics* [16], whose main topic is the use of interval arithmetic in order to obtain rigorous error bounds on numerical computations. Two detailed articles [17, 18] explain the pitfalls to avoid when doing floating-point computations.

A good introduction to computable numbers and their use in calculus is *Computable Calculus* by O Aberth [19]. For a practical application, see recent versions of the default calculator application in Android [20], or this online calculator.

References

[1] Clavel M, Durán F, Eker S, Lincoln P, Martí-Oliet N, Meseguer J and Talcott C 2007 *All About Maude—a High-Performance Logical Framework Lecture Notes in Computer Science* vol 4350 (Berlin: Springer)

[2] Turing A M 1937 On computable numbers, with an application to the "Entscheidungsproblem" *Proc. Lond. Math. Soc.* **42** 230–65

[3] de Lyon E N S 2012 The Turing Machine Comes True http://rubens.ens-lyon.fr/

[4] Centrum Wiskunde and Informatica 2012 A Turing Machine Built using LEGO http://www.legoturingmachine.org/

[5] Church A 1936 An unsolvable problem of elementary number theory *Am. J. Math.* **58** 345–63

[6] Minsky M L 1967 *Computation: Finite and Infinite Machines* (Upper Saddle River, NJ: Prentice-Hall)

[7] Moore C and Mertens S 2011 *The Nature of Computation* 1st edn (Oxford: Oxford University Press)

[8] Feynman R P 1982 Simulating physics with computers *Int. J. Theor. Phys.* **21** 467–88

[9] Diethelm K 2012 The limits of reproducibility in numerical simulation *Comput. Sci. Eng.* **14** 64–72

[10] Hopcroft J E, Motwani R and Ullman J D 2007 Introduction to Automata Theory *Languages, and Computation* 3rd edn (Englewood Cliffs, NJ: Prentice-Hall)

[11] Stuart T 2013 *Understanding Computation: From Simple Machines to Impossible Programs* 1st edn (Sebastopol, CA: O'Reilly)

[12] Hofstadter D R 1999 *Gödel, Escher, Bach: An Eternal Golden Braid* 20th anniversary edn (New York: Basic Books)

[13] Baader F and Nipkow T 1998 *Term Rewriting and All That* (New York: Cambridge University Press)

[14] Complexity Zoo http://complexityzoo.uwaterloo.ca/

[15] Muller J-M, Brisebarre N, de Dinechin F, Jeannerod C-P, Lefèvre V, Melquiond G, Revol N, Stehlé D and Torres S 2010 *Handbook of Floating-Point Arithmetic* (Boston, MA: Birkhäuser)

[16] Tucker W 2011 *Validated Numerics* (Princeton, NJ: Princeton University Press)

[17] Goldberg D 1991 What every computer scientist should know about floating-point arithmetic *ACM Comput. Surv.* **23** 5–48

[18] Toronto N and McCarthy J 2014 Practically accurate floating-point math *Comput. Sci. Eng.* **16** 80–95

[19] Aberth O 2001 *Computable Calculus* (New York: Academic)

[20] Boehm H-J 2017 Small-data computing: Correct calculator arithmetic *Commun. ACM* **60** 44–9

Computation in Science (Second Edition)
From concepts to practice
Konrad Hinsen

Chapter 4

Automating computation

In the last chapter, I described the transition from manual computations to formalized mechanical procedures for manipulating information. The next step is to delegate the application of these procedures to machines. In contrast to the automata of theoretical computer science, real machines have constraints, such as finite memory and limited speed, that need to be taken into account. Moreover, the interface between humans and computers requires careful consideration. We need to verify that our computers actually compute what we think they ought to compute, and we must find ways to extract scientific insight from the results of computations.

4.1 Computer architectures

There are many possible engineering solutions to the problem of building a machine that performs computations. The basic idea is to construct a physical realization of a dynamical system whose time evolution describes the progress of the computation. The exact physical nature of the realization does not matter. A computer could be made of mechanically moving parts or of reacting molecules. Today's computers are mainly based on semiconductor technology, and to a lesser degree on optical components.

A dynamical system is defined by a *state space* and a *time evolution rule*. A computer has a discrete state space containing the sequence of symbols that the computation processes. For the abstract Turing machine introduced in section 3.2, the state consists of the internal state plus the contents of the tape, which is a sequence of symbols from a fixed finite alphabet. In an electronic digital computer, the state consists of the internal state of the processor plus the contents of memory. This state can be broken down into *bits* (from 'binary digits'), i.e. symbols from a two-letter alphabet made up of '0' and '1'. A computer's time evolution rule defines for each possible state what the state at the next time step is. For the Turing machine, this rule is given by the instruction table. For a digital computer, it is defined by the processor's instruction set.

doi:10.1088/978-0-7503-3287-3ch4

To perform a computation, the initial state of the computer is prepared to contain the program being run and its input data. In today's dominant computer architecture, named *von Neumann architecture* after its inventor, John von Neumann, program and input data are both stored in memory, the difference between them being purely a matter of interpretation. Then the time evolution rule is applied repeatedly, until the state of the computer takes a value that indicates, using a suitable convention, that the computation is terminated. The result of the computation is then retrieved from the final state. This caricature view of computation is illustrated in figure 4.1.

4.1.1 Processors and working memory

The most universally adopted design choice in today's computers is the use of a binary representation, i.e. the computer's state is made up of bits. This choice is the reason for the ubiquitous use of powers of 2 in computing technology. Next on the universality scale comes the design principle of having a *processor* attached to *working memory*. The working memory is a list of memory locations, each of which is identified by a unique index called its *address*, which the processing unit can read out or modify in arbitrary order. The size of a memory location is called a *byte*, which in today's machines is equal to 8 bits. For efficiency, most processors can work on several consecutive memory locations in a single operation. Today the largest memory unit for a single operation is either 4 bytes ('32-bit machine') or 8 bytes ('64-bit machine'). The processor is also characterized by its *instruction set*, which associates a bit pattern with each operation that the processor can perform. A computer program is a sequence of such instructions stored in memory. The processor keeps track of its current position in the program via the address of the current instruction. It fetches the corresponding bit pattern from memory and executes the associated operation. It then continues with the next instruction from memory, unless the last operation explicitly requested something else.

These basic architectural choices have remained the same from the first electronic digital computers until today. The main changes have been in the size of working memory, processing speed, and the processor's instruction sets. As far as writing software is concerned, the most important change is that the speed of processors has

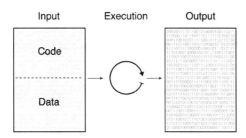

Figure 4.1. A caricature of computation: input data defines how execution proceeds, and execution leads to output. Input includes both the code and the data it processes, the distinction is irrelevant for the computer.

increased much more rapidly than the speed of working memory. In order to palliate the resulting speed penalty on memory use, engineers have added intermediate storage layers, known as *caches*, between the processor and the working memory. The first cache layer, which is closest to the processor, is the fastest but also the smallest. Two or three cache layers are commonly used. Whenever storage layer N requests data from storage layer $N + 1$, specialized circuitry tries to predict what data will be requested next, and moves it up in the cache layer hierarchy before it is actually being requested. Efficient programs must exploit these mechanisms by accessing data as much as possible in the order that the cache circuitry assumes. It can also be advantageous on modern computers to do more processing than necessary if this allows a reduction of the number of memory accesses [1].

4.1.2 Processor instruction sets

In scientific computing, it is almost never necessary to write programs directly in terms of the processor's instruction set. However, it is useful to have a general idea of what such an instruction set contains. Ultimately, all software run by a computer is expressed in terms of processor instructions. Software written in a programming language (see section 4.2) has to be translated to processor instructions before it can be executed. Understanding the processor's instruction set is useful for a better appreciation of which kind of operations are handled efficiently by the processor and which are not.

In the following, I will outline a typical modern processor's instruction set, without going into the details that vary between different processor types or between different generations of a processor family. An exact description of how every single instruction modifies a processor's internal state and working memory is provided by the manufacturer. For the most widely used processor architecture today, Intel's x86 series, this description fills 500 pages [2].

Processor instructions work on data items that are one, two, four, or eight bytes in size, assuming a 64-bit processor. They can be roughly divided into four categories:
- transfer to and from memory;
- integer arithmetic;
- bit-pattern manipulations;
- floating-point arithmetic.

The most basic memory transfer instructions copy data from the working memory into a processor register, or from a register to memory. A processor register is simply a memory area inside the processor, which can be accessed much faster than memory external to the processor. A copy instruction requires the address of the memory location, which is a bit pattern occupying four bytes on 32 bit processors and eight bytes on 64 bit processors. The size of this bit pattern defines the maximum amount of memory that a processor can work with. A major motivation for the transition from 32 bit to 64 bit architectures that started in the 1990s is in fact the possibility to use a larger working memory, a 32 bit processor being limited to 4 Gigabytes.

Integer arithmetic instructions interpret bit patterns as binary numbers and process them with an implied modulo operation in order to maintain a fixed-size representation for the result. The sum of two 32 bit integers a and b is thus another 32 bit integer $c = (a + b)$ mod 2^{32}. Put differently, c consists of the 32 least significant digits of the sum $a + b$. The full sum would require 33 bits of storage, the most significant digit is thus lost. The same principle applies to subtraction. Multiplication instructions typically take two N-bit factors and return a $2N$-bit product. Division of two integers produces two integer results, the quotient and the remainder. There is therefore no risk of overflow for a single multiplication or division, but when several arithmetic operations are done in sequence, it is inevitable to perform an explicit or implicit modulo operation as well, in order to stay within the limits of the data sizes that the processor can handle. As a simple example, the product of three N-bit factors a, b and c is computed as $((a \times b)$ mod $2^N) \times c$, i.e. with an added truncation to N bits of the intermediate product of a and b.

All arithmetic operations are usually provided for both *signed* and *unsigned* integers. An N-bit data item interpreted as an unsigned integer has a value range of 0 to $2^N - 1$. When interpreted as a signed integer, the value range is -2^{N-1} to $2^{N-1} - 1$. Negative numbers are handled via the *two's-complement* representation: a negative integer a is stored using the bit pattern for the positive integer $2^N + a$. The most significant bit thus contains the sign of the integer. These interpretations are illustrated in table 4.1 for two-bit integers.

Bit-pattern manipulations include bit-by-bit logical operations such as *and* or *xor*, but also operations such as 'shift all bits one position to the right'. The latter operation is an example of a bit-pattern manipulation that can also be considered an arithmetic operation, because it divides an integer by 2.

Floating-point arithmetic operations are the most complex ones in today's processors, and therefore also the slowest. They interpret four-byte data items as IEEE 754 single-precision binary floating-point numbers and eight-byte data items as IEEE 754 double-precision binary floating-point numbers, and perform arithmetic very close to the specifications in the IEEE 754 standard. Minor deviations from the standard are common, however, either because the processor design is older than the standard, or because a slightly different operation made the implementation simpler or more efficient. This is one reason for the common non-reproducibility of numerical computations (see section 5.2.6 and chapter 6).

Table 4.1. The interpretation of bit patterns as signed and unsigned integers.

Bit pattern	Unsigned	Signed
00	0	0
01	1	1
10	2	−2
11	3	−1

4.1.3 Special-purpose processors

What I have explained above is the design of today's general-purpose processors, of which every computer contains at least one. In addition, computers can contain special-purpose processors, which perform a more limited range of operations but at a much higher speed. The distinction between general-purpose and special-purpose processors is not a fundamental one but the result of economic considerations, which evolve over time. As an example, floating-point arithmetic was initially implemented in software, i.e. translated to an equivalent sequence of bit-pattern manipulation instructions. Because of their importance in many time-consuming computations, floating-point operations were then implemented in special-purpose processors, whose high cost was justified only for selected applications. With decreasing production costs, floating-point operations were finally integrated into most general-purpose processors.

Today's dominant type of special-purpose processor is the graphical processing unit (GPU). Its instruction set covers fundamental operations in the production of three-dimensional graphics, which it handles much faster than a general-purpose processor. Moreover, graphics processing often requires the same operation to be applied independently to a large number of data items (pixels on the screen), and GPUs can therefore execute many such operations in parallel. Finally, a GPU is located physically close to the graphics memory and has much faster access to it than the computer's main processor.

Since the type of operations required for processing graphics is also useful in other geometry-based computations, which occur in many scientific applications, GPUs have found uses that they were not initially designed for. Some GPU designs have subsequently evolved with non-graphics applications in mind. This is sometimes referred to as general-purpose computing on GPUs or GPGPU computing. The significant architectural differences between GPUs and general-purpose processors require software to be manually adapted for efficient GPGPU use.

4.1.4 Parallel computers

For a few decades, the speed of processors, and to a lesser degree memory, increased so rapidly that often the best way to speed up a lengthy computation was to wait for the next generation of computers. This speed increase was achieved by making chips smaller and run at a faster clock frequency. Physical limits, such as heat dissipation or even quantum effects such as tunneling, put an end to these approaches. Moreover, the increasing energy consumption of computers due to increasing clock frequencies became a problem. For these reasons, the quest for more computing performance started taking a different form. Parallel computing, an idea that had been around for a long time, started to be developed seriously around the beginning of the 21st century. Today, nearly all general-purpose computers in production, from smartphones to supercomputers, are parallel computers. The simplest way to exploit the parallelism in these machines is to run several completely independent programs at the same time. Each such program then behaves exactly as it would on a single-processor computer. The term 'parallel computing' is usually reserved for the coordinated use of multiple processors for performing a single computation.

The basic idea of parallel computing, i.e. having multiple processors work on different parts of a problem simultaneously, is simple, but obtaining an actual gain in overall performance is in general very difficult. In fact, the difficulties are exactly the same as for making teams of people perform efficiently. The overall task must be reorganized in such a way that it can be decomposed into independent sub-tasks that can be performed simultaneously, and a coordination strategy must be devised for ensuring that critical information is shared at the right time. Moreover, the coordination, called 'management' when referring to people, is a task of its own that requires competence and sufficient resources. In some areas of computational science, such as computational fluid dynamics, the problems are well understood and good solutions are available, with the result that parallel computation has become a routine technique, thanks to a long-term effort by a large and very motivated community. Unfortunately, parallelization strategies are not easily transferable from one application domain to another.

Parallelism has been introduced into computer architectures at three different levels, all of which can in principle be combined. The first level is the processor's instruction set. Instead of having each instruction process one data item, some instructions can perform the same operation on multiple data items in parallel. Most modern processors use this approach to some degree, and for GPUs it is the normal mode of operation.

The second level of parallelism consists of multiple processors sharing the same working memory. Such computers are called *multiprocessor* machines, or *multicore* machines if the processors are integrated on a single chip. Most commodity computers for desktop or mobile use are multicore machines, and use parallelism mainly for running the large number of completely independent processes related to tasks as different as graphics display and network communication. When used for speeding up scientific computations, all processors run the same program, which is written to behave somewhat differently on each of them. The general idea is that data processing tasks are divided into slices which are handed out to different processors. Coordination is performed through the shared working memory. The main limitation of this architecture is memory access. Even for a single processor, it is already slower than computation, and the difference increases when several processors have to share a single block of slow memory.

The third level of parallelism is the coordinated use of multiple processor-with-memory units, usually called *nodes*. Communication between nodes is handled through network connections. A computer consisting of multiple nodes with a fast communication network is called a *cluster*. This level of parallelism requires specially written software that contains both computations and the communication operations required for coordination. If the coordination overhead can be kept small, it is possible to use hundreds or even thousands of nodes together efficiently.

Parallelism inside the processor, i.e. level 1, involves nothing more than a suitable processor instruction set. Levels 2 and 3, however, represent a deviation from the view of a computer as a deterministic dynamical system evolving in discrete time steps. The individual processors are distinct dynamical systems, each having its own clock. If no measures are taken to carefully synchronize their computations, the result of a parallel computation can change as the result of small fluctuations in timing. Obtaining consistent and correct results from parallel computers is therefore a difficult task, without even considering the challenge of obtaining an actual performance increase over the use of a single processor.

4.2 Programming languages

The very first electronic digital computers required programmers to enter the bit patterns for instructions and input data via switches and buttons. This cumbersome method was quickly abandoned when computers started to be equipped with devices for the input and output of text. These were initially keyboards and printers, adapted from typewriters. The next step was text-mode terminals, which retained the keyboard but replaced the printer by a screen that was, however, restricted to displaying characters. In the course of time, terminals acquired more and more graphics capabilities, but fully graphical interfaces, and thus programming tools, became widely available only with personal computers in the 1980s.

The heritage of text-only interfaces between humans and computers is still visible in today's programming tools, in which *formal languages* play a very prominent role. Formal languages designed for writing programs are known as *programming languages*. Other formal languages serve for describing data, the best-known examples being HTML, XML, and JSON. The number of programming languages that have been created is huge and even hard to estimate. They include languages designed as practical tools as well as research languages and even languages developed purely for entertainment. I will limit the following discussion to programming languages used in computational science.

Programming languages are only one kind of tool in the toolbox of a programmer. Many of the other tools, such as text editors, have a rather obvious function. Two important but non-obvious tools, debuggers and profilers, are the topic of section 4.3. It is also worth pointing out that today's standard programmer's toolbox, in which programming languages take center stage, is largely a historical accident resulting from the restrictions of early computing hardware. As soon as interactive graphics became a possibility, people started to experiment with alternative ways to define computations. The earliest influential design was Sketchpad [3], which inspired, among others, Smalltalk [4], a programming system in which the overall code structure is defined using visual tools, with textual language only serving for short sequences of instructions.

Since all a computer understands is its processor's instruction set, the use of a programming language requires additional tools. There are basically two approaches to implementing a language. One approach, known as *compilation*, translates a textual program (known as *source code* because it is the information source in the compilation process) into an equivalent sequence of processor instructions, often called the program's *binaries* because they are not human-readable text (see also section 5.3.2). The other approach, known as *interpretation*, defines a virtual processor whose instruction set is the programming language, which is then simulated by a suitable program on the actual computer. The two approaches can be combined into a two-step setup: compilation of the input language to some intermediate formal language, which is then interpreted. Sometimes the transformation from program to processor instructions even proceeds via several intermediate representations. All transformation steps are themselves computations, and are performed by computer programs.

A programming language must provide at least three services:
- A notation for the data that a program works on.
- A notation for expressing algorithms.
- An abstraction mechanism for packaging data structures and/or algorithms in such a way that they can be used as building blocks in the construction of larger programs.

The abstraction mechanism is the most fundamental difference between a programming language and a processor instruction set. Computers do not need abstraction mechanisms, but humans do—I will come back to this in section 5.3. The most common abstraction mechanisms are data structures and functions, procedures, or subroutines. The latter are merely three different names for the same idea: a reusable piece of an algorithm. Object-oriented languages add objects and classes, whereas functional languages add higher-order functions. Less common and less standardized abstraction mechanisms include modules, logical relations, and syntax transformations. Identifying new abstraction mechanisms and evaluating them for practical applications is one of the main activities in programming language research. They are often inspired by, or developed in parallel to, formal models of computation of the type discussed in chapter 3.

4.2.1 Design choices

One reason for the large number of programming languages is the necessity to find a compromise between requirements that are often in conflict:
- The efficient use of resources, in particular time, memory, and energy, during program execution.
- The efficient use of resources for transforming the source code into processor instructions.
- The possibility to express complex computations in a notation that humans can understand and manipulate.
- The possibility to analyze a program effectively using some other program with the goal of verifying certain properties, in particular related to correctness.

I have listed these requirements in the order in which their importance was recognized over time. Early computers had a very limited capacity and could only handle simple computations. The top priority for programmers was to make the best use of the scarce machine resources. With increasing computing capacities and program sizes, clarity of notation was recognized as important for two reasons: to reduce the effort of writing programs, and to establish trust in the correctness of programs. Finally, with programs becoming still larger and more complex, and used for more and more safety-critical applications, source code inspection by human programmers became insufficient to ensure correctness, leading to the development of computational verification and validation tools.

Computational science differs from the more common engineering-type uses of computation in two important respects: First, scientists care more about the results of a computation than about the software that was used in obtaining these results. This has historically led to a widespread neglect of software quality. Second, computer programs are not only tools that are used to perform a computational task, but also the only existing notation for non-trivial computational models, as I have explained in detail in section 2.2. This means in particular that programs should be understandable not only by trained programmers, but also by the scientists that use them for doing research. This requirement should be reflected in the design of programming languages for science. So far this has not happened, mainly because the tool aspect of software is still dominant in most people's minds.

In the following I will discuss common conflicts between the requirements listed above. Different choices in each category explain much of the diversity that we have today among programming languages, and understanding these conflicts is important for making an informed choice of a programming language for a specific task.

Performance versus clarity and convenience
Programming languages are classified as 'low-level' if their notation for data and algorithms is close to the processor's instruction set. A typical low-level language has data types such as '32-bit signed integer', with operations on these data types corresponding to just a few processor instructions. At the other end of the spectrum, a 'high-level' language is based on the more abstract concepts that people use when describing computational tasks, for example 'integers' with no *a priori* restrictions on their values.

As an illustration of the difference, consider the simple computation y = x + 2 in the low-level language Fortran and the high-level language Python, assuming that in Fortran it is preceded by the declaration `integer*4 x, y`[1]. The Fortran code means: copy four bytes starting at the memory location called x to a processor register. Compute the sum modulo 2^{32} of the signed-integer interpretation of those four bytes and the constant 2, then copy the result to the four bytes of memory starting at the location called y. The similarly looking Python code has a very different meaning: obtain the addition function for the object that variable x refers to, call it with arguments x and a newly constructed integer object of value 2, and make the resulting integer object the new value of variable y, discarding whatever

---

[1] Fortran experts will note that the declaration `integer*4` is not part of any Fortran standard, although most compilers accept it. The standard does not make any promise about the handling of integer overflow either, but most compilers behave as I describe. Relying only on behavior defined in the standard would make my example much more complicated.

value it had before. The Fortran code typically corresponds to three processor instructions, whereas the Python code results in hundreds of instructions being executed, the exact number being difficult to estimate. On the other hand, when x has the value 2 147 483 647, the Fortran code will compute $y = -2\ 147\ 483\ 647$, which is most likely not what the programmer expected. The Python code will compute $y = 2\ 147\ 483\ 649$, applying the standard rules for integer arithmetic. The overhead of high-level languages is related to the cost of abstraction (see section 5.3.4) and reducing it is an active research subject in computer science.

The 'low-level' and 'high-level' categories do not cover the full spectrum of programming languages. A language can be somewhere in between the extremes, or span multiple levels. Moreover, since 'high-level' is defined by the use of abstract concepts from the application domain, it depends on the kind of problem one wants to solve. For numerical computations, the Python language can be considered high-level, but for manipulating graphs, it is only mid-level, because it requires the programmer to express graphs in terms of the simpler data structures it provides. The dependence of the 'high-level' label on the intended application domain has been the cause for much unproductive debate in comparing programming languages.

A final aspect of programming that needs to be considered is resource management. For a computer that executes a single instruction stream, the only resource to be managed is memory. Memory management becomes necessary because real computers, unlike the idealized Turing machine, have finite amounts of storage. A naive program that simply uses consecutive memory locations as it needs to store new values would thus quickly run out of available storage. A much better approach is to re-use the storage attributed to data that are no longer needed, i.e. intermediate values in the computation. This requires some book-keeping for deciding at which time it is safe to reclaim the storage space occupied by every piece of data. Some languages leave this task to the programmer, whereas others provide automatic memory management, most often based on a technique called *garbage collection*. This consists in periodically analyzing all references to stored data values, and mark data values without any surviving reference as garbage. The main disadvantage of automatic memory management is the associated overhead in terms of execution time. This needs to be offset against the two main disadvantages of manual memory management. First and foremost, manual memory management is difficult and thus prone to errors, whose consequences can be disastrous. Most of the security-related flaws in commonly used programs that are widely publicized are due to errors in memory management. Second, the insertion of memory management instructions into the program source code makes the latter less understandable and more difficult to modify. The trade-off is thus between clarity, reliability and convenience on one hand and performance on the other.

In parallel computers, processor time is another resource that needs to be managed. The main motivation for parallel computing is to have the final result earlier than with a single processor. It is thus important to assign subtasks to the individual processors in such a way that the total computational charge is equally distributed, a management task known as *load balancing*. Bad load balancing leads to situations in which some processors have to wait, performing no useful work, until some other processor has finished its subtask. Another important management task is to divide the total computation into smaller tasks in such a way that the overhead for synchronization and data exchange between the processors is minimized. Like memory management, processor management can be performed automatically or left to the programmer. But unlike automatic memory management, which is a mature technology, automatic parallelization is still a research subject. Today's practically usable programming languages (as opposed to languages developed for research in computer science) provide at best some support for helping the programmer to manage parallelism.

The choice of manual versus automatic resource management is *a priori* independent of the low-to-high level scale. However, most languages are either 'performance oriented', i.e. low-level with manual memory management, or 'clarity oriented', i.e. high-level with automatic memory management. These two major priorities are often also reflected in how a language is implemented and which development tools are provided for the implementations. Performance-oriented languages are typically implemented as optimizing compilers that convert a program into a processor instructions for a specific computer. Programmers must run this compiler explicitly before being able to run their own program. Clarity-oriented languages are usually implemented as interpreters or as hybrid combinations of interpreters and just-in-time compilers, which do their work in the background when a program is executed, making them mostly invisible to the programmer. Finally, the priorities in language design also influence the ecosystem of program libraries that are written in a specific language. Libraries in performance-oriented language tend to be more specific to a precise task and optimized for it, whereas libraries in clarity-oriented languages tend to be more flexible and thus more easily reusable for different tasks.

The most popular performance-oriented languages in scientific computing are, in historical order, Fortran, C, and C++. The popularity of clarity-oriented languages is more domain-specific. Matlab is an early example of a clarity-oriented language that became popular for applications that rely on linear algebra and signal processing. The R language has attracted many scientists who apply advanced statistics, whereas the Python language comes closest to an all-purpose scientific high-level language. An example for a low-level language with automatic memory management is Java, which has found some uses in scientific computing but is much more popular for business applications. There are also broad-spectrum languages that try to support the goals of performance and clarity simultaneously, though they end up having to make compromises: 2 147 483 647 + 2 can be either 2 147 483 647 or −2 147 483 647, but not both. Common Lisp, whose use in scientific computing is mostly limited to computer algebra systems, is a broad-spectrum language that gives priority to clarity. Julia, a recent language for numerical applications, chooses performance first.

Verifiability versus simplicity

The fourth requirement for a programming language, the possibility to verify program properties by a mechanical analysis of the source code, is particularly important for the construction of large software systems, whose complexity exceeds what a competent programmer can handle mentally. The properties that one would like to check are related to the correctness of the program. Ideally, one would prove that the result of the program is correct for all possible inputs. Unfortunately, that requires a precise specification of these results in terms of the inputs, which is almost as much information as a program for computing them. In practice, mechanical proofs are much less ambitious, verifying simple properties of intermediate or final values. The only verification approach that is widely used by today's programming languages is known as *static type checking*.

The general idea of static type checking is to associate a tag, called a *type*, with every value in a program. Operations applied to these values are annotated with the expected types of their inputs and the type of their results. A type checker, which is typically an integral part of a compiler, then verifies that the program is a valid combination of operations with respect to the language's type compatibility rules. The qualifier 'static' specifies that this verification happens by inspecting the source code, i.e. without actually executing the program. This is important because executing the program might take a very long time, at worst an infinite amount of time. Moreover, a bug might show up only with specific and rarely used input values, and can then be detected only after years of use, by the user of the program rather than by its developer.

In principle there is an enormous choice of possible type tags for use in a type checker. In practice, most languages use their data abstractions (see section 5.3.2) as types. Typical type tags are therefore '32-bit integer', 'unicode character string' or 'array of double-precision floating point numbers'. The main reason for this choice is that this information is by construction always available for every piece of data, making it straightforward to check. This is not the case for more application-oriented types such as 'positive number': it is very hard to prove that a function returning a number will actually return a *positive* number for any permitted combination input values. A second reason for using data abstractions as types is their utility for program optimization by the compiler. As an example, knowing the data representation of the result of some library function, the compiler can allocate memory for this result without first having to compute it. Statically typed languages are therefore often associated with better performance. Some languages use static type declarations almost exclusively for optimization purposes. The C language, for example, permits programmers to bypass all type compatibility rules, thereby reducing the utility of type checking for ensuring correctness.

Static type systems have been one of the most passionately discussed features of programming languages for many years, with no consensus in sight. Most arguments presented for or against static type checking are based on their proponents' personal experience, and are therefore subjective and domain dependent. A common but very abstract argument for static type checking is that any mechanism for verifying program correctness is a desirable feature in a programming language.

This argument overlooks that every language feature comes at a cost, because a more complex language specification implies a steeper learning curve. The impact of static type checking on the robustness and performance of the code, on human productivity, and other relevant aspects should be expected to depend on many factors. Unfortunately, that also makes it difficult to explore empirically, although empirical validation would be the best antidote to passionate exchanges of subjective impressions.

Static type systems range from simple to elaborate. Simple type systems are easy to learn, but can quickly get in the way of the programmer by forbidding useful constructs. For example, a type system that considers 'list of integers' and 'list of character strings' to be entirely different types requires a programmer to write generic list processing functions, such as computing the length of a list, more than once. A more sophisticated type system avoids such restrictions using parametric types like 'list of values of type X'. However, as type systems become more sophisticated, they also become more difficult to master. At the extreme, for a strongly type-oriented language such as Haskell, most of the effort in learning the language comes from the complexity of the type system.

Languages without static typing come in two varieties. *Untyped* languages treat all values identically, much like processor instructions treat all memory contents as plain bit patterns. Such languages are rare, one example being Tcl, in which all data is represented by character strings. *Dynamically typed* languages distinguish different kinds of data using tags, but they store the tags along with the data in memory and check them when executing each operation. Performing the checks at run-time obviously reduces overall program performance, and storing the tags increases the memory footprint of a program.

The choice between static and dynamic typing thus implies a trade-off between robustness on one hand and simplicity of the language and the programs written in it on the other hand. Static type checking is useful, and thus worth paying the price of reduced simplicity, if typical programmer mistakes have a high chance of leading to a type error that can be caught by the type checker. Whether this is true or not depends both on the type system and on the kind of programs one wants to write, and perhaps even on the programmer.

In scientific computing, we find mainly two language categories: dynamically typed clarity-oriented languages (Python, R, Julia, Matlab, ...), and statically typed performance-oriented languages (C, C++, Fortran, Java, ...). In the latter category, most type systems are of the performance-motivated kind. This suggests that scientific programmers are mostly not convinced of the utility of static type checking for ensuring program correctness, contrary to many professional software engineers and to the majority of programming language researchers.

Computing results versus developing software tools
Another compromise that affects the choice of a programming language is due to the different motivations that make scientists write code. One of them is exploring datasets, or computational models and methods, and documenting such analyses in publications. The focus in these activities is on the datasets, models, and methods,

with code often being specialized for a single application. The other main motivation is producing software tools for use in future research projects, requiring code to be general, usable by others, and often also more efficient.

Computational exploration includes data analysis, performing simulations, querying databases, and many other tasks. It can be done interactively, or by executing an automated sequence of processing steps. An automated sequence of processing steps is of course nothing else but a computer program, written in a programming language. What sets it apart from a software tool is that it fully specifies a computation, including all parameters and input data. It's the final element that ties together all the software tools that contribute to answering a scientific question. Programs written for automated computational exploration are usually called *scripts*, *notebooks*, or *workflows*.

There is no consensus on what exactly a script is, and how it differs from other types of programs. The most agreed-on characteristic is that a script is a simple program contained in a single file, which can be run immediately, i.e. without requiring preparatory steps such as compilation. Scripts typically call other programs to do most of the work, and thus act as a kind of glue between larger and more generally applicable pieces of software. In its simplest form, a script is simply a list of commands, each of which specifies which program to run and which input parameters to supply to it. Scripts can also contain simple control flow components such as conditional execution or loops. Programming languages designed for writing scripts have compactness and clarity as high priorities.

The term 'workflow' is even less clearly defined than 'script'. The general idea of a workflow is to define a computation by a collection of data transformation rules rather than by a specifying the order of operations. Workflows thus resemble the term rewriting systems described in section 3.1 with terms replaced by files containing data. A workflow can, for example, apply a processing step to all files matching a name pattern in a given directory. The first workflow tool, make, was written in the 1970s for automating the compilation of complex software. A make workflow defines rules such as 'to compile a file whose name ends in .c, run the program gcc and give it the filename as input'. Executing the workflow in a given directory then compiles all files matching the specified filename pattern. The original make is still widely used for its original purpose, but also by scientists for automating computational explorations. Many other workflow tools have been developed later. Workflow systems tend to be pragmatic, aiming at doing specific kinds of computations well rather than trying to be all-purpose tools. It is therefore important to choose a workflow system after a careful analysis of requirements. For example, some workflow systems can distribute individual tasks among multiple machines, but only for specific architectures of computing resources.

Computational notebooks are an evolution of scripts that adds two features: better documentation facilities, and the inclusion of computed results. A notebook is a text document with embedded code snippets and embedded results. The text parts are usually written in a lightweight markup language, such as Markdown, and can in more sophisticated notebook systems also include images or mathematical formulas. Code snippets are written in the same programming languages commonly used for scripts. The notebook manager inserts the results after the code snippet when the latter is executed, either as text or as graphics, e.g. for plots. Although from a strictly computational point of view, a notebook is no different from a script, there is significant added value from the point of view of communication between authors and readers. A well-written notebook reads like a story that includes computations and their results. Some notebooks (e.g. Jupyter) also store the computed results together with the documentation and code cells, whereas others (e.g. R Markdown) do not. Both choices have their advantages: storing the results makes them accessible without the need to re-run the computation, but it also creates a hybrid file mixing inputs and outputs, which is difficult to use with source code management tools such as version control systems.

Although notebooks have proven to be an excellent medium for documenting computational work, they suffer from the same limitations as scripts, in particular that the whole computation must fit into a single file. Notebooks even impose stricter constraints because conditional execution and loops can only be used inside a single code snippet. More complex computations, such as those typically managed by workflows, cannot be adequately performed in notebooks.

Scripts and notebooks use programming languages of the clarity-oriented kind (see section 4.2.1), with Python, R, and Julia being popular choices at this time. Workflows differ from ordinary programs in that their control flow is determined by files external to the workflow. As a consequence, workflow languages look very different from standard programming languages. Some workflow managers do not use a text-based language at all, but instead represent workflows as graphs of tasks and/or data files that are manipulated using visual tools.

Computational exploration and tool development are only the extreme points on a continuum. Intermediate scenarios arise for several reasons. New models and methods are developed and tested in exploratory mode, but then often migrate into software tools. The script that performs an analysis on a specific dataset is turned into a tool that takes the dataset as an input parameter. The design of new software tools often requires building prototypes before deciding on a specification for a high-quality implementation, and the prototypes resemble computational explorations in being ephemeral code. New ideas flow from method development via prototypes into optimized software tools. There is thus a permanent need to migrate code from scripts, notebooks, and workflows into software tools. Unfortunately, there is at this time no good technology to support this migration. Scientists have to choose between time-consuming reimplementation and the slow accretion of scripts and workflows into code mazes that are difficult to maintain.

Generality versus adequacy for a specific purpose
As I have explained in section 3.3, all formal languages that are Turing-complete can express the same computations, and to this date nobody has found a formal language that can express more computations than a Turing-complete one. Turing-completeness thus ensures maximal generality in a programming language. However, making it possible to express every possible computation is not sufficient to make it convenient in practice. In fact, if Turing-completeness were all we cared

about, we would write programs directly using a processor's instruction set. Programming languages are all about convenience for humans.

For many tasks, Turing-completeness is not a requirement, and for some, it may actually be a disadvantage. The generality of a Turing-complete language comes at a price: it is possible to write useless programs, i.e. programs that never terminate, and it is not possible to detect such programs by an inspection of their source code. This means that a particularly nasty kind of mistake is impossible to detect by analyzing a program. Non-termination is merely the best-known property that is undetectable in a Turing-complete language, but there are many others. In general, there is a conflict between the generality of a language and the possibility to verify properties of a program written in it. Some computer scientists advocate the 'principle of least power': a program should ideally be written in a language with just as much expressive power as strictly necessary, in order to maximize the possibilities of analyzing it.

Shifting the focus from computability to convenience, we also find sources of tension between generality and convenience for specific applications. If you want to write programs for processing DNA sequences, your ideal language would have only two data types: DNA sequences and integers. Any additional data type, such as character strings or floating-point numbers, would only add potential confusion and a source of errors. A general-purpose language, on the other hand, does not include a data type for DNA sequences, which would be useful for only a small fraction of its users. The conventional resolution of this conflict is writing a library in a general-purpose language that implements DNA sequences with their associated operations. While this achieves the important goal of making DNA sequences convenient to work with, it does not address the other problems of general-purpose languages: (1) the many features that are not required for processing DNA sequences create sources of errors, (2) the generality of the language makes programs more difficult to analyze, and (3) the implementation of DNA sequences as a library has to respect the constraints of the language's generality-oriented syntax, usually making programs more verbose than they would have to be.

A recent approach to solving these problems is the definition of *domain-specific languages*. Such a language does not aim for generality. It is designed for processing a narrowly defined range of data, providing only language features that are useful in this context. A domain-specific language can be designed from scratch, or as a variant of a general-purpose language that is both extended and restricted. Domain-specific languages are not yet widely used in scientific computing, but first examples for tasks such as defining differential equations [5], particle-based simulations [6], or probabilistic models [7], illustrate the potential of this approach.

The idea of domain-specific languages has interesting parallels to scientific notation. In principle, every scientific model could be expressed using a sufficiently fundamental mathematical formalism. It has been shown that all of today's mathematics can be expressed in the language of set theory, meaning that one could in principle write Newton's laws of motion, or the bond graph of a macromolecule, in terms of sets and a few fundamental operations of sets. Set theory thus is the mathematics analog of a general-purpose programming language. Defining additional set operations for convenience is the analog of writing libraries in that language. However, practical scientific notation is very different. Neither differential equations nor molecular structures are written with any reference to sets. The fact that functions and graphs are ultimately defined in terms of sets is almost completely irrelevant to how they are used as building blocks in scientific models. The notations of calculus and graph theory are thus mathematical equivalents of domain-specific languages.

Standardization versus individualism
A major difference between information and matter is the enormous flexibility of information. While the design of physical devices is subject to many constraints that often impose a particular engineering solution to a problem, information is largely free from such constraints. Given a programming language or a data format, it is trivial to derive many others from it that are neither better nor worse, perhaps even fully equivalent, but different enough to be incompatible.

The desire to distinguish oneself from one's competitors has motivated both computer manufacturers and programming language researchers to introduce variants of existing programming languages with minor differences. For widely used languages, such a period of diversification has in the past often been followed by a standardization effort in which the various stakeholders try to find a compromise language definition. While standardization is beneficial to the programmer who seeks stability and portability, and to the researcher who cares about long-term reproducibility (see chapter 6), its impact on programming language design is often deleterious, the two main symptoms being ambiguity and feature bloat.

Ambiguity results in a program having different meanings on different computing platforms The C language is particularly concerned by this problem, because the strong motivation for permitting optimizations has pushed the standardization committees to introduce additional intentional ambiguities [8]. As an example, the declaration `int` n means 'make n an integer of the size that the processor handles most efficiently'. Writing C programs that produce the same results on all computers therefore requires a significant effort.

Feature bloat leads to large language specifications that both programmers and language implementers find hard to learn and understand entirely. Programmers tend to limit themselves to language subsets, but are then often forced to deal with the language parts they tried to ignore when faced with compiler error messages or when having to work with code written by someone else. C++ and Common Lisp are examples for languages suffering from feature bloat.

Most formal standards in computing technology, not only for programming languages but also for data languages such as XML, or library interfaces such as OpenGL, were initiated in the 20th century. More recent technology tends to be defined by a single implementation whose evolution is controlled by a single company or a single Open Source community. This allows for faster evolution, but also makes software foundations more fragile for users that are not part of the institutions that control them. Much software has been lost to incompatible changes in subsequent version of the Windows operating system, or in the transition from version 2 to version 3 of the Python language. I will discuss this phenomenon in more detail in section 6.7.

4.2.2 Social and psychological aspects

Anyone who is in contact with software developers, scientific or otherwise, soon notices how passionate discussions about programming languages can be. It is difficult to explain this emotional investment by the technical aspects of programming languages that I have outlined above. Very few people are passionate about technicalities. The explanation must be found in the non-technical aspects of programming languages, and which are important both in choosing a language and in evaluating what is written about languages.

Programming languages, like human languages, are a notation to express thoughts. Compared to human languages, programming languages are much more limited, as all they can express is algorithms and data structures. In return, programming languages are much more precise and compact. But it is worth looking at the similarities as well. Becoming 'fluent' in a programming language involves not only learning its rules, but also becoming familiar with idioms for expressing frequent code structures, and with the writing styles of the well-respected authors who use the same language. All this represents a serious effort, which many people try to justify to themselves and others retroactively by exaggerating the advantages of the languages they know compared to those they would have to learn. Moreover, programmers who use the same language form a community inside which communication and collaboration are easier than with people from outside the community. Belonging to such a community can easily become part of a person's identity, creating a motivation to 'defend' the community's language against perceived criticism, even when the criticism is justified.

When choosing a programming language, the community behind the language deserves as much scrutiny as the language itself. Doing any non-trivial work in a language implies joining its community to some degree. Even if you only write small scripts yourself, you will use much code written by others. Quite probably you will have to ask for help with such code. Even more probably, you will have to read and understand it. At some point, you may well want to contribute back to the community, for example by publishing some of your code. It is therefore important to check if you are at ease being in contact with that community. Is it open to new members? Do its values resonate with yours? Are there other members who work on similar problems as yourself?

Finally, there may also be language features that may be more in line with your preferences than features in other languages. Do you prefer a simple language, even though it requires you to write more verbose programs? Or are you an adept of compact code, willing to learn a large number of idioms to get there? Are you attracted by a style resembling mathematical equations, or by a style imitating natural languages? Would you rather use punctuation or reserved words as syntactical markers? Such preferences probably depend on your culture and education, perhaps even on your personality. You can probably force yourself to learn any language, but you will be more productive if you choose one that you like. To cite once more Donald Knuth: 'The enjoyment of one's tools is an essential ingredient of successful work.' [9]

4.3 Observing program execution

A program plus its input data fully define what happens during the execution of a computation. In principle it is therefore sufficient to read the program text in order to know what is going to happen. Unfortunately, this is not true at all in practice. With all but the most trivial programs, what happens when the program is run the first time is not at all what its author had expected. Obtaining the expected program behavior typically requires several iterations of modifying the program and observing its behavior.

The most obvious way to observe a program's behavior is inspecting its output. If you want to observe some intermediate result that is not part of the output, you can modify the program to *make* it part of the output, an approach colloquially known as 'inserting print statements'. It's an obvious approach, but not a very efficient one. Every time you add or remove a print statement, you have to re-run the program from the start, and depending on your chosen language you may have to recompile it first. This makes it tedious to observe a program's behavior in detail, and as a consequence most scientists prefer to observe only as much as strictly necessary, contrary to what one would expect a good scientist to do.

There are two kinds of tools designed for observing program execution: *debuggers* help with observing *what* a computation does, and *profilers* facilitate the observation of the *performance* of a program.

4.3.1 Debuggers: watching execution unfold

The name 'debugger' suggests a tool meant primarily for finding mistakes in programs, which are called 'bugs' in programmer jargon. This is unfortunate, because a good debugger is equally useful for exploring the inner workings of correct code.

A debugger provides a dashboard that controls program execution. It allows its user to define *breakpoints*, which are locations in the code where program execution is interrupted to allow inspection. Conditions can be added to each breakpoint, yielding something like 'stop at the entry to this function if the first argument is equal to 21'. When the condition is satisfied, the debugger shows the code around the current position and lets the user inspect the values of variables. Errors during program execution are treated as breakpoints as well. The exact functionalities for defining breakpoints and inspecting the program state vary enormously between debuggers. The ease of use of debuggers is also highly variable. Many scientists quickly give up on debuggers after a first experience with a bad one, but it's worth persevering until you find a good one.

Debuggers tend to be closely integrated with compilers or interpreters, and their functionality closely related to the language(s) implemented by these tools. Users of highly dynamic languages such as Smalltalk or Python tend to have the best debuggers at their disposal. At the other extreme, strongly performance-oriented languages (see section 4.2.1) typically have poorer debugging support, because the optimizations made by their compilers interfere with interactive execution. However, debugging support is not a feature of a language, but of an implementation. Even for traditionally performance-oriented languages such as Fortran or C, some implementations provide better debugging support than others.

4.3.2 Profilers: measuring execution time

Performance is an important characteristic for many scientific applications, because some scientific programs can run for weeks or even months. Designing and implementing efficient programs is an art by itself. Unfortunately, experience has shown that humans are as bad at predicting the performance of their code as they are at predicting its exact behavior. Very often, scientists set out to rewrite a part of their program in view of improving its performance, only to be disappointed by meager results in the end. The reason is that the parts of the program that contribute most to execution time are not those its authors had expected to be performance-critical. It is therefore important to *measure* performance, rather than to make educated guesses.

The tools for making such measurements are called profilers. Like debuggers, they exist for most implementations of most programming language, but their functionality and ease of use is highly variable. Unlike debuggers, profilers also require the user to learn *how* each profiler does its work. Experimentalists are well aware that any measurement modifies the quantity being measured. The measurement of program execution times is no exception, and therefore the user of a profiler needs to understand what exactly is being measured and what side effects the measurement can have, in order to avoid misinterpretation of the results.

Most profilers use two types of measurements: event interception, and statistical sampling. In event interception, the profiler modifies the program in order to be informed of events such as entering or leaving a function. It then records the event with a timestamp. In statistical sampling, the profiler interrupts the program at regular intervals and checks which part of the code was active at the time of the interrupt. The output of a profiler includes various forms of timings ('how much time was spent in total in function X'), but also simple execution counts ('how often was line 50 of module X executed'). Timings can also be shown for the call graph ('how much time was spent in total in function X, including all other functions it called').

4.4 Software engineering

Software engineering is a discipline aiming at the development of techniques for the construction of good software. The meaning of 'good software' depends on what the software is going to be used for, but it generally includes criteria such as doing its job correctly, behaving reasonably in unforeseen circumstances, being ergonomic to use by its human operators, not wasting computational resources, and being adaptable to evolving requirements. Compared to other engineering disciplines, software engineering is still young and immature, relying more on trial and error approaches and on the intuition of its practitioners than on empirical studies and well-understood principles. A major difficulty of software engineering is the rapid change in computing technologies: the effective lifetime on the market of software development tools and techniques is often so short that a careful empirical study of its properties cannot be completed before it disappears.

In view of this immaturity of software engineering in general, it is not surprising that software engineering approaches to the specific needs of scientific computing are almost completely absent. The main distinctive feature of scientific computing is the lack of a clear separation between software developers and software users. The user-programmer dichotomy is replaced by a circular continuum of tasks and roles that people can assume in computational science, as illustrated in figure 4.2. At the most user-like point (lower-right quadrant), we have the scientist using software that applies well-understood methods as a research tool, for example in simulation work or in data analysis. This scientist requires no more than a precise description of the models and methods that the software applies, and which he or she presumably knows already. A scientist who evaluates, modifies, or develops scientific models and methods (lower-left quadrant) needs a much better understanding of and control over software, but would still like to be shielded from scientifically irrelevant technical details such as resource management and differences between computational platforms When model and method development reaches the point where it makes sense to perform large-scale computations (top-left quadrant), computational efficiency begins to matter, which usually means that software must be specialized to a specific type of computer. This stage is most similar to the job description of a programmer in other application domains. Finally, in the top-right quadrant, we have the adaptation of software tools to new research problems, a task that requires an in-depth understanding of the software architecture well beyond that of a plain

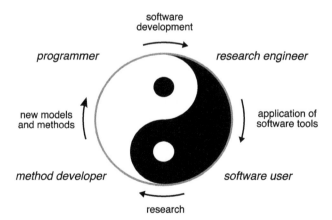

Figure 4.2. The interplay of research and software development in computational science. The white surface represents the transformation of scientific ideas into computational tools, the black surface represents the derivation of scientific insight from computation. The opposite-colored dots inside each surface serve as a reminder that each aspect requires a small dose of the other one.

user. Overall, the left-hand side of the circle is about new computational methods, whereas the right-hand side is about new applications. Furthermore, the upper part could be labeled 'software development', with the lower part being called 'scientific research'.

In fact, this is not very different from how science interacts with engineering in technologies other than computing. The process leading from the discovery of stimulated light emission via the development of high-performance lasers to the use of lasers as light sources for new research has followed the same pattern. Experimental scientists have collaborated with engineers and technicians in this way for more than a century. But the development of scientific computing was driven by theoreticians, who have no tradition of collaborating with experts who focus on a different aspect of the problem. Until the 1980s, most progress in theoretical science was made by individuals or by small teams of scientists with a shared educational background, which included a mastery of the mathematical techniques needed for working with their models. The continued application of this working style has led to the current situation in which most scientists use computational methods and write scientific software without any formal training in computation or software development, whereas those who specialize in the software development end of the spectrum find it difficult to obtain recognition and thus employment in academia. This is starting to change with the increasing recognition of research software engineers as an important competence profile for scientific research.

Another common difference between scientific and business-oriented software development is the organizational structure of the development teams. Business software is often produced by employees of a single company, whereas scientific software tends to be created by a lose network of research groups for whom software development is only one activity among others, and hardly ever the primary one. This is similar to the 'bazaar' style of development in many Open Source projects, for example the Linux operating system [10]. Since the Open Source philosophy is also similar in spirit to the requirements of transparency and reproducibility in science, many tools and software engineering techniques from the Open Source community have been adopted by computational scientists [11]

4.5 Further reading

Donald Knuth's multi-volume opus *The Art of Computer Programming* [12] is a treasure trove for many of the topics discussed in this book. His fictitious MIX processor is a good way to learn about processor instructions sets without getting lost in the technical details of any specific real processor type.

A classic textbook that still remains an excellent introduction into the concepts of programming and programming languages is *The Structure and Interpretation of Computer Programs* by Abelson and Sussman [13]. Its use of examples from science and engineering make it particularly suitable for computational scientists. The book is also available online, as is a series of video lectures based on it.

Books explaining computing techniques to scientists are still rare and usually limit themselves to teaching a programming language. A much wider range of topics, including the management of data and source code, is covered in *Effective Computation in Physics* by Scopatz and Huff [14], using the Python language for all examples. Langtangen's *A Primer on Scientific Programming with Python* [15] is a good example for computing skills being taught in parallel with numerical methods rather than as a separate topic.

References

[1] Alted F 2010 Why modern CPUs are starving and what can be done about it *Comput. Sci. Eng.* **12** 68–71

[2] Intel Corporation 2015 *Intel 64 and IA-32 Architectures Software Developers Manual, volume 2: Instruction Set Reference*

[3] Sutherland I 1963 Sketchpad: a man-machine graphical communication system *PhD Thesis* MIT

[4] Goldberg A and Robson D 1989 *Smalltalk-80:* The Language (Addison-Wesley Series in Computer Science) (Reading, MA: Addison-Wesley)

[5] Logg A, Mardal K-A and Wells G (ed) 2012 *Automated Solution of Differential Equations by the Finite Element Method Lecture Notes in Computational Science and Engineering* vol 84 (Berlin: Springer)

[6] Awile O, Mitrovic M, Reboux S and Sbalzarini I F 2013 A domain-specific programming language for particle simulations on distributed-memory parallel computers *Proc. III Int. Conf. on Particle-based Methods* http://mosaic.mpi-cbg.de/docs/Awile2013b.pdf

[7] Stucki S, Amin N, Jonnalagedda M and Rompf T 2013 What are the odds?: Probabilistic programming in scala *Proc. of the 4th Workshop on Scala, SCALA '13* (New York: ACM) pp 11:1–9 https://dl.acm.org/doi/10.1145/2489837.2489848

[8] Regehr J *A Guide to Undefined Behavior in C and C++* http://blog.regehr.org/archives/213

[9] Knuth D E 1997 *The Art of Computer Programming, Volume 2: Seminumerical Algorithms* 3rd edn (Boston, MA: Addison-Wesley)

[10] Raymond E 1999 *The cathedral & the bazaar* (Sebastopol, CA: O'Reilly)

[11] Millman K J and Perez F 2014 Developing open source scientific practice *Implementing Reproducible Research* ed V Stodden, F Leisch and R D Peng (Boca Raton, FL: CRC Press)

[12] Knuth D E 1997 *The Art of Computer Programming, Volume 1: Fundamental Algorithms* 3rd edn (Redwood City, CA: Addison Wesley)

[13] Abelson H and Sussman G J 1996 *Structure and Interpretation of Computer Programs* (Cambridge, MA: MIT Press)

[14] Scopatz A and Huff K D 2015 *Effective Computation in Physics* (Sebastopol, CA: O'Reilly)

[15] Langtangen H P 2016 *A Primer on Scientific Programming with Python, Texts in Computational Science and Engineering* vol 6 (Berlin: Springer)

IOP Publishing

Computation in Science (Second Edition)
From concepts to practice
Konrad Hinsen

Chapter 5

Taming complexity

The complexity of today's software, data, and computational models is one of the major challenges for every computational scientist. Reliability is of prime importance for any scientific result. But how can one trust the result of a computation so complex that verifying it in detail is impossible? Mistakes can easily creep in, and can easily remain unnoticed.

This issue is of course not specific to computations. Mistakes are easily made in applying mathematics, and experiments are subject to many potential sources of error. However, for the traditional techniques of science, useful verification and validation approaches have evolved over centuries and are taught to students. For writing software and applying computational methods, comparative techniques are much less advanced and rarely even mentioned in science curricula. Moreover, the complexity of software introduces sources of error that are qualitatively different from those of the past and that most scientists are not even prepared to recognize. The few highly publicized cases of mistakes in computational science [1] are probably just the tip of the iceberg; it must be assumed that many more published computational results are wrong because of mistakes in the development or application of scientific software.

In this chapter, I will explain the sources of error that are specific to software, and present some techniques that have been found useful in dealing with this problem. For simplicity, I will use the term 'software development' in a very wide sense that includes every act of formalizing a computational protocol. Many computational scientists may not think of themselves as software developers, but at least on a modest scale, they really are. Software complexity thus concerns everyone doing computational science.

It is unfortunate that the term 'complexity' is used with different meanings in the context of computational science. This chapter is about the complexity of computer programs. It is unrelated to computational complexity (Section 3.5) and only slightly related to Kolmogorov complexity (Section 2.2.4) and the computational study of complex systems (section 2.2.3). It is best to consider all of these concepts as distinct.

5.1 Chaos and complexity in computation

In section 4.1, I have described computers as dynamical systems whose state is the contents of the computer's memory, and whose time evolution rule is defined by the processor's instruction set. The program and input data make up the initial state of the system, and the result of the computation is part of the final state, after the time evolution rule has been applied a large number of times.

An important feature of this dynamical system, whose consequences are not yet sufficiently appreciated, is that it exhibits chaotic behavior. Chaos, like complexity, is a concept that has so far no consensual rigorous definition. What characterizes chaos is a strong sensitivity of a system's behavior on initial conditions: small changes in these conditions can cause arbitrarily large changes in future states. Applied to computers, this means that the result of a computation depends strongly on the initial state (program plus input data), to the point that a small change in this initial state can change the result beyond any predictable bound. This happens because small changes are amplified in the course of the computation. The smallest possible change in the initial state is flipping a single bit in memory. The impact of such a flip can be small, for example if the bit happens to represent the least significant digit of an input number. At the other extreme, a one-bit flip in a processor instruction can crash the program, leading to no result at all. In between these two extremes, a one-bit flip can lead to results that differ from the correct result in arbitrary ways. The worst case is a result that is wrong but looks credible. Such mistakes have a good chance of going unnoticed.

A simple example for such chaotic behavior is shown in figure 5.1, which I have adapted from a lecture by Gérard Berry [2]. Travel directions on a Manhattan-style grid of streets are encoded by a very simple language that consists of only three distinct one-letter instructions: S: go straight on at the next crossing, L: turn left, R: turn right. The smallest possible change in such an instruction sequence is the replacement of a single letter. A correct instruction sequence plus two minimally modified versions are shown in the figure, together with the resulting itineraries. The end points of the modified itineraries are in no way close to the correct one.

Computers being physical devices with limited reliability, single-bit flips in memory can actually occur, either as a result of hardware defects, or of external perturbations (thermal fluctuations, radiation, etc). However, today's computers are extraordinarily reliable, to the point that these sources of error can safely be ignored in scientific computing, with the exception of extremely long-running computations on large supercomputers. However, human mistakes in preparing programs and input data have exactly the same consequences. Changing a single letter in the source code of a program is not very different from flipping a bit in memory.

The complexity of today's software only adds to the difficulty of verifying its behavior. Programs consisting of millions of processor instructions are very common. These instructions are not thrown together at random, as would be, say,

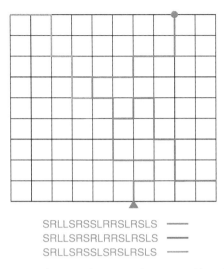

SRLLSRSSLRRSLRSLS ——
SRLLSRSRLRRSLRSLS ——
SRLLSRSSLSRSLRSLS ——

Figure 5.1. Travel itineraries on a Manhattan-style map can be expressed in a simple programming language. Each letter encodes the instructions for one crossing. S: straight on, L: turn left, R: turn right. The blue instruction sequence encodes the blue itinerary, which correctly leads from the starting point (triangle) to the destination (circle), presumably respecting one-way streets and other constraints. The red and orange itineraries are the result of single-letter changes in the code. These small changes lead to large deviations from the destination point.

the molecules in a glass of water. They are carefully assembled into a functioning whole, like the parts of a clockwork. However, a complex mechanical watch consists of only a few hundred parts. A car is made of tens of thousands of parts. Most scientific instruments are somewhere in between, and thus have many fewer parts than a typical piece of software.

The chaotic nature of computation stands in stark contrast to lab equipment for experimental science, which is carefully designed to be tolerant to the small imperfections that are inevitable in the manufacture of physical devices. A production defect in a microscope can lead to blurred images, but it will not add two legs to the image of a fly. In contrast, a computer program for generating synthetic images of flies[1] might do exactly that as a consequence of a small mistake. After 400 years of making and using microscopes, backed up by a well-tested theory of optics, the symptoms of bad quality in these instruments are well understood. An experienced microscopist knows how to evaluate the quality of a new microscope, and knows if an observed artifact could potentially be caused by a defect in the instrument. In contrast, even the most experienced computer programmer or computational scientist cannot decide easily if a given computer program does, even approximately, what it is supposed to do, either by looking at the program or by looking at a sample of its results. Experienced programmers know that mistakes are often discovered accidentally, and fully understood only after a careful analysis

---

[1] Or the genetic code that defines the actual body of a fly!

tracing a wrong result back to its sources. For these reasons, careful verification and validation of software and computational results is particularly important.

Many computational scientists like to adopt the point of view that complex computations, in particular simulations (see section 2.2.3), are a form of experiment. This point of view has its origins in analog computing (see section 1.3), for which digital computing is seen as a more convenient replacement. However, this point of views neglects the fact that analog computers, like other lab devices, are carefully designed to avoid chaotic behavior, unless it happens to be a characteristic feature of the natural system being studied. Digital computers are thus not convenient replacements for analog computers, but fundamentally different devices.

5.2 Verification, validation, and testing

Some of the methods that scientists use to verify and validate their experimental or theoretical findings can be applied to computational results as well. Moreover, software engineers have come up with various techniques for verifying software in general. In this section, I will describe the approaches that have proven most useful in the practice of computational science, in particular for the small to medium size projects that most scientists are involved in. However, these techniques cannot be considered sufficient, as surprising mistakes continue to be identified in software that was developed using state of the art methods.

The biggest problem with verification and validation in computational science is that it is often not even attempted. Computational scientists, like computer users in general, place too much confidence in their software. We tend to consider the results of a computation correct unless there is a good reason to suspect a mistake. We also tend to consider a piece of software reliable if it is widely used by other scientists. In fact, we treat software just like any piece of equipment or machinery, in the lab or at home. However, this attitude does not take into account two particularities of software. First, the complexity and chaotic behavior discussed in section 5.1, which make it difficult to anticipate the possible consequences of a mistake. Second, the immaturity of computing technology in general. Consider how often your computer crashes, how often it asks you to install security-critical software updates, or how much time is wasted at scientific conferences when computers refuse to communicate with video projectors. Compare with the frequency of malfunction in cars, refrigerators, or lab spectrometers. We should treat software with much more suspicion than products of mature technologies. Ask yourself regularly why you should believe the numbers your computer spits out. Inquire about any software you plan to use. How was it verified and validated by its authors? Has it been verified and validated independently by other users? Can you verify and validate it yourself?

5.2.1 Verification versus validation

The distinction between *verification* and *validation* is well established in many engineering fields, but less so in scientific research. Verification operates at a technical level, asking questions such as 'Have mistakes been made?', 'Was our standard protocol followed?', or 'Do we get the expected results for routine tests?'.

Verification questions typically have clear yes/no answers, and one would expect all domain experts to agree about them. Validation, on the other hand, is about the adequacy of a technique or method in a particular application context. Typical questions asked are 'Is this type of experiment appropriate for answering the scientific question?', 'Are the approximations that were made justified for the system being studied?', or 'Do we get the same result if environmental conditions change a bit?'. The answers require scientific judgment, and different scientists might well disagree about them while still recognizing each other's expertise.

For computational techniques, verification focuses on two questions: (1) Does the software correctly implement the models and methods that the researchers wish to apply? (2) Has the software been used correctly? Validation has a less narrow focus, inquiring about the choices of models, methods, and parameters. A particularly important type of validation question in computational science concerns the robustness of methods and tools: How precisely must some input parameter be specified? Does it make a difference if I compile this program using `gcc` or `clang`? Robustness is also an issue in experimental methods, of course. One might wonder, for example, if the outcome of an experiment strongly depends on ambient temperature. But software and computational methods tend to involve a much larger number of seemingly arbitrary choices that must be made to move on, but have no obvious relation to the scientific question being explored.

5.2.2 Independent repetition

A simple yet very effective strategy for verification or validation is independent repetition. Experimental scientists are used to running an experiment several times, to check for variations in the results. Theoreticians often re-do their on-paper calculations a few days later, just to check for mistakes. If they want an even tighter check, they ask a colleague to re-do their work. On a larger scale, independent replication of complete studies is one of the cornerstones of the scientific method.

When applied to computation, it is the human work that needs to be repeated, not the computer's. There is little point in running the same program with the same input data more than once. Instead, we'd like to vary everything that we believe should *not* influence our results, in order to evaluate the robustness of a computational method and the reliability of the human operators. Use a different computer. Use two different pieces of software that perform the same task. Have the repetition done by a different person. When writing software for a research project, have two people write the code independently, using different languages or libraries, and then compare the results. For small-to-medium size scripts, this is quite a feasible approach. Independent repetition is a very effective strategy not only for detecting programming mistakes, but also for acquiring a more precise understanding of the computation. Quite often, a disagreement in independently produced results turns out to be the consequence of different assumptions made when translating an informal description into precise code. This is a case of computing contributing to understanding, as mentioned in section 1.2.

The main practical difficulty with independent repetition is deciding what to do if the results do not agree. In my experience, this is the rule rather than the exception for any computational work that requires writing new software. One should, of course, track down the cause of the disagreement. But this can be very difficult for computational work that relies on software written by someone else. With proprietary software, tracking down the cause of the difference can be impossible. An important precaution to reduce such difficulties is to use only software whose source code is publicly available for inspection. Moreover, prefer software with an active developer and user community that you can turn to for help in case of unexpected behavior. Finally, start doing independent repetition as early as possible in the project, as mistakes in small programs are much easier to pinpoint and correct than in larger ones.

5.2.3 Testing

The most common verification approach for software, scientific or otherwise, goes by the simple name of *testing*. The basic idea of testing is to construct simple problems whose correct solutions are known by some other means. It is then straightforward to verify that the program finds a solution that is identical or sufficiently close. Of course, one simple problem is not sufficient to verify a program designed for solving much less simple problems. Multiple test cases are required, and ensuring that the test cases taken together really probe all parts of the software is one of the hardest tasks in testing. Software tools provide support that often includes *code coverage*: the tool checks which lines in the program have been executed at least once while running the test suite. While not a guarantee for the absence of mistakes (no amount of testing can provide such a guarantee), watching out for code coverage in a test suite helps to avoid overlooking parts of the code when testing. The existence of a test suite with good code coverage is today considered a major criterion when evaluating the quality of a piece of software.

Tests are the archetype of verification as opposed to validation: their outcome is binary (passed/failed) and determined automatically by the computer. The possibility of automation makes verification a much more powerful approach for computational techniques than for experimental ones. Most programming languages have specific support tools that facilitate the management of a large number of tests, and in particular produce a report summarizing the results of a complete test suit. Becoming familiar with such a tool is definitely worth the effort.

The best moment to start writing tests is while writing the program being tested. There is even a school of thought, called *test-driven development* (TDD), that advocates writing tests *before* writing the program. One reason for testing early is, once again, that finding and fixing problems is easiest while a program is small. In addition, tests are very convenient during program development, because they permit checking that a modification of the program, such as an enhancement or an optimization, does not introduce any obvious mistakes. The kind of tests that are most useful during development are *unit tests*, which I will come back to in section 5.3.

5.2.4 Redundancy

Let us have another look at the travel direction example from figure 5.1. When we give someone travel directions in real life, we do not use a three-letter programming language. We describe the itinerary in sentences that contain more than just a minimal set of instructions. For example, we might say 'go straight on for about 200 m, until you arrive at 5th street, then turn right and continue straight on until you see a grocery store on the left'. The additional information is redundant, because it is not strictly required to get to the destination. However, it is very useful for validation. If, after moving straight on for 200 m, we do not arrive at 5th street, something has gone wrong. We can then backtrack and try to correct our itinerary, much earlier than if we followed a long instruction sequence to the end to discover that we did not get to the right place.

Redundancy can also be used effectively for the verification of software. The general idea is to add pieces of code that verify known but non-obvious properties of intermediate values. You might know, for example, that the result of a computation must be a positive number. You can then add a statement, called an *assertion*, that verifies this property and produces an error message if it is not satisfied. Some programming languages have specific statements for this purpose. For example, in the Python language, `assert x > 0` will stop the program with an error message if the condition `x > 0` is not satisfied. A more elaborate variant of this idea is the use of *contracts*, which are sets of conditions that must be satisfied at the beginning and end of a procedure.

Redundant information in the form of assertions or contracts also serves as additional documentation for the code. Compared to a comment, it has the important advantage that the reader knows that these properties are actually being checked as the program is run. The only disadvantage is that this run-time checking adds some overhead to program execution. Often it is so small that it is not worth worrying about, either because evaluating an assertion is cheap, or because it is not done frequently. Expensive checks can be made optional, leaving the choice of including them or not to the user.

5.2.5 Proving the correctness of software

A verification technique that is not yet used routinely in computational science is *formal verification*, which is a mathematical proof of the correctness of a program. Formal verification starts from a *formal specification*, which defines precisely what the program is supposed to compute. A specification differs from the program itself in that it does not necessarily say *how* a result is computed, nor is it concerned with efficiency. As a simple example, the specification for a program that sorts a list of words alphabetically simply states that the result must be a sorted list having the same elements as the input list.

Given a specification, a program called a *proof assistant* is used to construct a logical proof that shows that the result of the program conforms to the specification for all possible inputs. Today's proof assistants provide only little help with actually finding such a proof, but they can verify proofs constructed by humans, and they keep track of what remains to be proven. Proving a program correct remains at this time a difficult and lengthy process, and the method is therefore applied only for software whose correctness is crucial, such as airplane control software. Nevertheless, there are some encouraging first uses in computational science [3].

5.2.6 The pitfalls of numerical computation

Numerical computations, which are very common in computational science, have the reputation of being very difficult to verify and validate. As I have pointed out in section 2.1.2, numerical methods in science are always approximations, and most commonly, as for my example of solving Newton's equations for the solar system, obtained after multiple approximation steps. At each step, there are typically many similar approximations to choose from. Differential equations can be discretized in different ways, systems of equations can be solved using different algorithms, and solutions can be computed to various levels of precision.

Exploring the impact of all these approximations on the final results is an exploration of the robustness of the overall method, and thus a form of validation according to the definition I have given in section 5.2. One way to do this is independent repetition, as described in section 5.2.2: letting two researchers, or two teams, write code meant to solve the same problem, and compare the results. This is, however, feasible only for small projects. Another way to explore robustness is varying parameters and algorithms in a more systematic fashion, but this is easier said than done.

Numerical analysts have therefore developed specific techniques and tools for studying the robustness of numerical algorithms. The oldest one is *interval arithmetic*. It consists of replacing values by ranges of values, described for example by an upper and a lower bound. Each operation computes the range of possible results from the ranges given for its inputs. In practice, a lot of effort is required to avoid needlessly overestimating the result range, which would falsely suggest the algorithm to lack robustness. Another technique is the injection of random noise into each numerical operation, and studying the distribution of the final results of the algorithm. This is known as *stochastic arithmetic* or *Monte Carlo arithmetic*.

Unfortunately, there is a further source of trouble with numerical computations: floating-point arithmetic. As I have explained in section 3.6.1, compilers for all of today's popular programming languages re-arrange floating-point operations with the goal of improving program performance, even if this modification changes the outcomes of the operations. Moreover, all programming languages in practical use present a simplified view of floating-point arithmetic to the programmer, in which many subtleties of the IEEE 754 become inaccessible. The result of a program using floating-point arithmetic is therefore not fully defined by its source code. It depends on choices made by processor designers and compiler writers. The differences that are introduced are small at the level of an individual operation, but can quickly be amplified by accumulation over many operations.

In view of the other inevitable approximations in numerical algorithms, the impact of incomplete result specification by the program source code is usually negligible for practical computations. It does, however, have a strong impact on *testing* numerical code. Testing is supposed to check the correctness of the code. All allowed interpretations of the code by a compiler must therefore make a test pass, whereas every incorrect result must make it fail. Since this is impossible to achieve without a monumental effort in writing each single test case, most tests for numerical code allow generous error margins for the results, to prevent the test from failing in a different environment. This greatly reduces the value of testing, because mistakes in the code can go unnoticed.

5.3 Abstraction

The principle that prevention is better than cure also applies to software development. While verification and validation are always necessary to ensure the reliability of software, and to convince others of it, it is clearly preferable not to make mistakes than to find mistakes after the fact. While no technique can guarantee a program that is free of mistakes, some approaches to designing software result in fewer mistakes than others. Unfortunately, such observations are for now based mainly on anecdotal evidence, as software engineering has not yet widely adopted the scientific method in exploring the effectiveness of its techniques.

One basic principle of software design is common to all engineering disciplines: *abstraction*. A car may consist of tens of thousands of pieces, when decomposed down to the last screw, but a car designer thinks in terms of functional units such as engines, gear boxes, and wheels. Designing an engine is considered a separate task, done by somebody else. The same engine can be used in different cars, and the same car model can be equipped with different engines. This is possible because each of the functional units in a car can be specified independently of all the others, as long as a relatively small set of interface conditions is respected [4]. The engine and the gear box are directly coupled, leading to strict compatibility conditions. On the other hand, the engine is completely independent from the seats. Changing the color of the seats will not cause the engine to stall. This principle of composing a system from parts with well-defined interfaces is an important ingredient in software design as well.

Abstraction stipulates that parts should have a simple functional specification that does not depend on how they are constructed internally. The car engine is an example of such an abstract part. A car designer can use an engine without knowing how many screws it contains, or what material the pistons are made of. Abstractions can be made at various levels in the design of a complex system, leading to a *hierarchy* with multiple *levels of abstractions*. A car engine is itself designed in terms of modular components, many of which have an internal structure of their own, making them lower-level abstractions. Examples are pistons or spark plugs.

The reason why engineers make heavy use of abstraction is that this is how the human brain handles complex systems and processes. We use abstractions all the time without even noticing. 'Opening a bottle' is an abstraction that, depending on the type of bottle, translates to 'unscrew the cap' or 'pull the cork'. Each of these actions is in turn another abstraction, which ultimately translates to a complex sequence of movements involving many joints and muscles, guided by visual feedback. Most of us would probably not recognize the action of unscrewing a cap in a detailed list of the corresponding movements. Our brains need abstractions in order to keep the description of any action simple at the top level. For the same reason, a complex program must be structured by abstractions in order to be comprehensible to a human reader.

The principles of abstraction are the same in software engineering as in other branches of engineering, but applying them productively to software remains much more difficult. The main reason for this is that software engineering is such a young discipline, compared to the design of machines, which builds on knowledge accumulated over hundreds of years. Another reason is that the laws of physics impose severe constraints on machine design, whereas information can be shaped and transformed very freely. For every design choice in software engineering, it is straightforward to find variants that are neither better nor worse, just different. As a consequence of these particularities, we do not yet have the software equivalents of standardized and well-understood construction parts such as screws, bricks, or wheels.

In terms of difficulty, there is an enormous difference between using well-designed abstractions and designing good new abstractions. Most children figure out rapidly how to use Lego bricks to build a house, but few people ever come close in their lifetime to inventing something like the Lego brick. The same is true for software: composing high-quality libraries into a program that solves a specific problem is well within the reach of a scientist without much programming experience, but designing software libraries for use in larger projects requires some combination of talent, motivation, and many years of practice [5]. The following overview of abstraction techniques is therefore no more than a guide through the jungle of software developers' jargon. It is the equivalent of a summary of the rules of chess, rather than a tutorial for becoming a good chess player. The relation between the different keywords is illustrated in figure 5.2.

5.3.1 Program abstractions

As I have mentioned in section 4.2, support for abstractions is one of the essential services provided by a programming language. The most basic and most important abstraction mechanism, available in all popular programming languages, is called a *procedure*, a *function*, or a *subroutine*. All these terms denote a section of code with a well-defined interface through which it can be used as a building block in larger programs. The interface of a procedure describes what information it requires and what information it provides. A procedure typically has explicit inputs, called

Figure 5.2. The different types of abstraction in software engineering.

arguments or parameters, that must be provided for executing it. In addition, a procedure may directly access information from elsewhere, for example global variables (i.e. variables defined outside of the procedure), a database accessed through a network, data from a file, or interactive user input. The information produced by a procedure likewise falls into two categories: explicit return values and effects. Return values are retrieved immediately for further processing by the code that calls a procedure. The effects consist of everything that changes in the computer or its environment when the procedure is executed: text being printed to the terminal, data being written to a file, global variables being modified, etc.

A general rule in software design is 'explicit is better than implicit'. It is better to feed information to procedures through explicit parameters, and retrieve the result of its computations via explicit return values, rather than have the procedure consult and modify global variables or disk files. When you read a piece of code that calls procedures, you see the information flowing in and out explicitly, whereas the use of other information resources is hidden. Of course, every useful program *must* at some point read input from the outside world and deposit its results somewhere. Such operations should be concentrated in as few places (procedures) as possible. As for global variables, they should ideally be avoided completely, as they are a frequent source of hard-to-find mistakes. I will come back to this problem in section 5.4.

A procedure does not automatically define a useful abstraction. What characterizes an abstraction is that it performs a well-defined function and that it can be used as a 'black box' whenever that function is required, without the user having to pay attention to its internal workings. Whether or not a procedure is a useful abstraction is not a formal question that can be verified by some analysis tool. Abstractions are not made for computers but for humans, and their utility depends on how well human programmers understand them.

In section 5.2.3, I briefly mentioned unit tests as the most useful kind of tests during scientific software development. Unit tests are tests for small units of software, rather than for entire software packages. The 'units' that are being tested are in fact the units of abstraction, such as procedures. A unit test is a very small piece of 'client code' that uses a unit of abstraction to compute an already known result for verification. An obvious advantage of a unit test, compared to a full-program test, is that it can be performed much earlier, as soon as a testable unit is finished. A less obvious but equally important advantage is that writing the test is an exercise in writing client code. If writing unit tests turns out to be difficult, the abstraction is perhaps not well designed. Finally, a set of unit tests is an important part of the documentation of the unit, because it illustrates how it is meant to be used and for which use cases it has been verified.

A procedure typically uses other procedures as building blocks, and thus becomes part of a multi-level hierarchy of abstractions. The programming language being used defines the bottom layer in that hierarchy, and the complete program being written is the top layer. Moreover, procedures can be used as data items, and thus passed into other procedures as arguments or returned from them as results, although not all programming languages allow such techniques. A typical use case would be a procedure that computes the definite integral of a mathematical function, and takes as one argument another procedure that computes the function to be integrated. Procedures taking other procedures as arguments are called *higher-order* procedures and play an important role in a programming style called *functional programming*, on which I will say a bit more in section 5.4.

5.3.2 Data abstractions

Ultimately, all data in a computer are stored as sequences of bits, just as all program code becomes a sequence of processor instructions. Neither representation is of much direct interest to computational scientists. The kinds of data we want to process with the help of a computer are images, DNA sequences, molecular structures, mathematical equations, and other domain-specific scientific information. Somebody must decide how to represent all this information in terms of bits. This defines the task of data abstraction, which proceeds in a hierarchical way exactly like program abstraction: the bottom layer is bits, the top layer is a description of the data we want to work with, and in between we have more or less generic data abstractions such as numbers or sets.

Data abstractions are particularly important in computational science because data lie at the heart of science. In figure 2.1, all the boxes are data, whereas programs correspond to the arrows between the boxes. For scientific research, the data matter more than the programs used to process them, because all conclusions are based on data. For this reason, data abstractions for science should be designed carefully to be precise and clear, and documented thoroughly to ensure that the data can be correctly interpreted by others, now and in the future.

Unfortunately, data abstraction is a topic that has been very much neglected not only in scientific computing, but also by computing technology in general. The focus of technological development has been on software seen as a tool to do things. The data that the software processes takes a secondary role, and the decision of how to represent data in terms of bits is taken by tool developers according to criteria of convenience. As a result, much of our data is stored in so-called *proprietary* formats, i.e. formats defined by the developers of a specific piece of software, which is often not even documented. The most ubiquitous proprietary file format is probably the 'doc' format defined by the word processing software 'Microsoft Word', but there are also many highly domain-specific proprietary formats in computational science. These formats quickly become an obstacle to creative research, and should best be avoided.

A fundamental difference between data and program abstractions is related to the fact that data lead a double life: different design criteria apply to data used *inside* a program and to data stored *outside* a program. Inside a program, data abstractions are implemented as *data structures*, whereas outside a program they become *data formats*, usually defined as parts of *file formats*. Both data structures and data formats ultimately define how data are represented as sequences of bits. Data structures are designed together with the algorithms that process them, and are formally defined in program source code along with program abstractions. Data formats are designed for compact storage, fast reading and writing, and ease of processing, i.e. ease of developing software that reads and writes the data. They are often described using human languages, sometimes complemented by a reference implementation, which is simple software that reads or writes the format. More recently, special formal languages have been created for describing data formats, a well-known example being XML Schema [6].

In practice, data structures and data formats are never specified at the bit level, just like programs are not written in terms of processor instructions. The elementary data structures provided by programming languages, such as numbers, text strings, or arrays, are the lowest level of description that programmers work with in practice. Most programming languages also provide abstraction mechanisms, such as structures or objects, to define higher-level data structures. Such definitions can then become parts of software libraries, exactly like program abstractions.

For file formats, one of the oldest and most widely used abstractions is the *text file*, defined as a sequence of characters. The characters are then mapped to bits via an *encoding* in terms of a *character set*. The earliest portable character encoding was the American Standard Code for Information Interchange (ASCII), which is still commonly used for scientific data because of its simplicity. In an ASCII file, each character occupies one byte, of which only seven bits are used, allowing for 128 distinct characters. Since this is not enough to cover the many writing systems used around the world, variations of and alternatives to ASCII have flourished for many years, to be ultimately subsumed by the *Unicode* standard in the 1990s. Today, Unicode covers almost all of the world's writing systems, including some extinct ones, and is almost exclusively used for representing text on the World Wide Web. There are, however, multiple encodings for Unicode in common use. Due to the large number of characters, four bytes are required to uniquely define a single one. The different encodings are compression schemes designed for a compact representation of common subsets of the full Unicode character set. For languages using variants of the Latin script, the most popular encoding is called UTF-8, for '8-bit Unicode Transformation Format'. It is an extension of the ASCII format that uses the 128 values unused by ASCII to encode the rest of Unicode in terms of sequences of two to four bytes. The price to pay for this compact representation is the variable number of bytes per character, which makes processing text files more complicated.

Many common file formats are defined in terms of text files, for example the increasingly popular so-called lightweight markup languages such as Markdown, Org-mode, or reStructuredText. Much scientific software also uses text formats for input and output data. The big advantage of text files is that they can be inspected and modified using standard tools available on every modern computer. The most important kind of tool is the text editor, but there are many other common tools for searching, filtering, or transforming text files. This vast tool ecosystem is the main reason why text files should be preferred for data storage unless there is a very good reason to choose a *binary* file format, which is by definition anything that is not a text format. The main reason for preferring binary formats is a more compact data representation, which also permits faster processing. Binary formats are therefore most frequently used for very large datasets.

One layer above characters or bytes, there are several widely used generic file formats for structured data. They manage a tree-like structure in which each item is accessible via a path from the root of the tree. For text files, the most popular structured data formats are XML [6] and JSON [7], but there are others that have become dominant in specific domains, such as STAR [8] in crystallography. Several binary formats for structured data are in use for managing large datasets. FITS, the flexible image transport system [9], is a rather simple format for storing arrays, initially intended for storing images and widely used by astronomers. HDF5, the fifth version of the hierarchical data format [10], offers a much more flexible data model with good performance at the price of a more complex file format. Using any of these structured formats yields two important advantages over designing a complete format specification at the byte or character level: a considerably simplified data format specification, and an equally simplified implementation in software because ready-made libraries exist to process these formats.

Finally, a *data model* defines the general characteristics of a data abstraction, independently of the technical considerations that influence the design of data structures and formats. A data model for gray-scale images, for example, specifies that an image is represented by a two-dimensional array of integer numbers in the range 0...63, with 0 representing black and 63 representing white. Implementing this data model as a data structure or data format requires two additional specifications: how to represent a two-dimensional array, and how to represent integers in the range 0...63. Since the smallest unit of memory that a typical processor can access is a byte, and the smallest unit one can read efficiently from a disk file is a byte as well, efficiency considerations suggest representing each integer number by one byte, even though this wastes 25% of the memory space (64 possible values can be encoded in six bits, whereas a byte is eight bits). Alternatively, we can give priority to memory efficiency and choose to store four consecutive pixel values, i.e. 24 bits, in three consecutive bytes, at the price of less efficient access to the data. Designers can make different choices in different situations. The important point is that all implementations of a data model can always be converted to each other, without loss of information. A community of developers can therefore agree on a data model and retain much freedom in choosing data structures and formats according to their specific needs.

Data models are also important in the early design phase of software design and for its documentation. In fact, data models are related to data structures and formats in the same way as algorithms relate to the procedures that implement them (see figure 5.2). Algorithms and data models completely define a computation, but leave open the technical details of making a specific physical device perform it. Bad data abstractions are often the result of defining a data structure or format without first thinking about the data model. The risk is that implementation details become the top priority in the design, whereas criteria such as suitability for all intended purposes are easily overlooked.

5.3.3 Object-oriented programming

Up to here, I have discussed program and data abstractions as if they were independent. Quite often they are not. Program abstractions process data and thus depend on data abstractions. A procedure that enhances the contrast in a digital image needs to access the data representing that image. The algorithm being used depends on the data model for the image, and the procedure that implements the algorithm is written specifically for the image data structure.

Let us assume that we have a software library for image processing, and we want to use it to write a program that analyses digital micrographs. The library contains a procedure for reading an image from a file, and a couple of procedures to process and analyze images. That is in fact all we need—we do not really care about the data abstraction that the library defines for images. For making an image processing tool, all we need to know is that there is *some* data abstraction for images, and most importantly what we can *do* with images using program abstractions from the library.

This observation is the basis for a software development approach known as *object-oriented programming*. It was developed in the 1960s, but became popular only in the 1990s. Today, many programming languages support object-oriented programming explicitly with specific abstraction mechanisms. Some languages, e.g. Java, even enforce an object-oriented approach by not proposing any abstraction mechanism outside of the object-oriented paradigm. Many people with a superficial knowledge of software engineering therefore believe that object-oriented methods are the key to good software design. This is clearly not true. Experience has shown that it is quite possible to write bad object-oriented software, and also good software using other paradigms. The nature of the abstraction mechanism being used is in fact less important than a good understanding of how to apply it. Object-oriented programming is a useful paradigm to know for a computational scientist, because it is a good fit for many scientific programming tasks, but it is not a panacea that magically solves all software design problems.

In object-oriented terminology, an *object* is simply a piece of data. Each object is an *instance* of a *class*. The class is the central abstraction mechanism. A class is a package combining a data abstraction with associated program abstractions that define what one can do with the instances of the class. In an object-oriented approach, the image abstraction corresponds to a class that defines (1) an appropriate data structure (the two-dimensional array of integers in the range $0\ldots63$) and (2) a set of procedures (which are called *methods* when they are part of a class) for manipulating and analyzing images. The important point is that a user of that class does not need to know anything about the data structure or the internals of the methods. The data abstraction is fully defined by its behavior, i.e. by the operations proposed by the methods. For the designer of the abstraction, this creates more freedom to modify the internals of the implementation, and thus adapt it to new computer systems or different use cases, without breaking client code that depends on it.

In an object-oriented design, it is common to have multiple related classes that define variants or specializations of some data abstraction. Object-oriented programming languages propose *inheritance* mechanisms to facilitate the definition of such class families. Another technique for exploiting similarities among multiple classes is *polymorphism*, which consists in defining a method in several classes in order to allow client code to use the method without having to know to which of these classes an object belongs. This makes it possible to write code that can be used identically on different (but related) data types.

One of the attractions of the object-oriented approach is that there are some useful general guidelines for choosing good abstractions, i.e. classes. One of them is: write down a concise description of the problem you want to solve in plain English. Identify the key concepts in that description, and divide them into nouns and verbs. Turn the nouns into classes, the verbs into methods. Applied to scientific computing, such an analysis leads to classes representing physical objects such as atoms or lasers, and mathematical entities such as numbers or graphs, which are indeed the kind of classes used in object-oriented scientific software.

5.3.4 The cost of abstraction

Structuring programs in terms of abstractions is a necessity in dealing with complexity. However, it comes at a price: a well-structured program can be both longer and slower than a program performing the same computation in an optimized but unstructured way. As a simple example, consider common mathematical functions such as sine or logarithm. They are perfect candidates for program abstractions, implemented as procedures. Many more complex mathematical functions can be expressed from a few fundamental ones. However, when you have to compute both the sine and the cosine of the same numbers, calling two completely separate procedures for sine and cosine is inefficient. A single procedure computing both functions together could exploit relations between them, such as $\sin^2(x) + \cos^2(x) = 1$, and thus do less computational work. Such situations arise very frequently, creating a tension between optimizing a program for human understanding or for computational efficiency.

The cost of abstraction is also an important design criterion for programming languages, which I have already outlined in section 4.2.1. High-level languages insert more layers of abstraction between the programmer and the processor than low-level languages, favoring human understanding over computational efficiency. Many current research and development efforts aim at reducing the cost of abstraction, both at the language level and at the level of software libraries and application programs. One example of such techniques is *inlining* of procedures: a compiler replaces a call to a procedure by a copy of the procedure itself, and then looks for repetitive computations that could be performed only once. Another example is *just-in-time compilation*, which defers the generation of processor instructions for a procedure to the moment when it is executed. At execution time, a compiler knows not only the procedure's source code, but also the actual input data to the procedure, allowing optimization for concrete special cases rather than for unspecified abstractions.

5.4 Managing state

As you know by now (see section 4.1), computers are dynamical systems whose state is the contents of memory. The term 'memory' should be understood in a very wide sense. It is not just the working memory directly connected to the processor, but also includes all information storage devices that the computer communicates with: hard disks and USB sticks, but also cloud storage accessed via a network. The state of a typical desktop computer is therefore quite large, its order of magnitude being 10^{12} bytes. As I have explained in section 5.1, changing a single bit in this state has unpredictable long-term consequences that include the possibility of a crash as well as the possibility of a wrong result.

As every experienced programmer knows all too well, state corruption is one of the most frequent causes of problems in computing. When a programmer sets out to track down the cause of an incorrect behavior in a program, an activity known as *debugging*, he or she often discovers that some memory cell in the computer had been changed by a part of the program that was not supposed to change it. Such mistakes are particularly difficult to track down, because they require the program's execution to be followed step by step. The economic cost of the consequences of state corruption in computer programs is hard to estimate because it exceeds the mere cost of finding and fixing these mistakes. As an illustration, major security flaws in widely used computer programs make their way into the news every few months. Almost all of these security flaws are due to a mistake in state management. If such a mistake leads to the theft of millions of credit card numbers, the damage can be millions of euros. In scientific computing, security issues are rare and the economic impact of mistakes is hard to estimate, but the scientific damage from wrong published results can be quite important [1].

Some frequent state corruption cases can be identified even without much technical expertise. Whenever you reboot your computer because it behaves strangely, the cause is state corruption. Rebooting, after all, is nothing but re-initializing the computer's memory contents to a known good state. If that becomes necessary, the prior state was in some way invalid. Similarly, when you re-install your operating system to fix your computer, you can deduce that the state of its hard disk had been corrupted.

State corruption happens when a program modifies the contents of some memory area incorrectly. It is always the result of a mistake in a program, and in the vast majority of cases, the mistake is in an operation that explicitly writes data into a memory location, i.e. an operation that assigns a new value to a variable or to an element of a composite data structure. The frequency of this type of mistake suggests that humans are not very good at foreseeing the consequences of changing the contents of memory locations. In view of the chaotic behavior of computers (see section 5.1), this is not really surprising. Over the last decades, much work on programming languages and software engineering techniques has concentrated on making such mistakes less frequent. Before looking at some of them, I will discuss what state itself looks like in a computer program—it is always helpful to know your enemy.

5.4.1 Identifying state in a program

Until now I have described state at the level of the computing hardware, where it consists of the contents of memory cells. In programming languages, state has a different appearance. The simplest form of state is found in Fortran 77: a program's state consists of the values of all its scalar variables and of all the elements of all arrays. For simplicity, I will use the term 'variable' from now on to refer to anything whose value can change, i.e. both scalar variables and array elements. Each variable has a value at each step in execution. This value remains the same unless it is changed by an assignment statement. This means that in a Fortran 77 program, state corruption can only be caused by assignment statements.

Languages such as C or Fortran 90 that offer pointers and dynamic memory allocation require a much more complicated description of state. Obviously the contents of the dynamically allocated storage must be included in the total state of a program, but that is only the first step. Each such storage block can itself contain pointers to other storage blocks. The neat distinction between variables and values disappears: the value of a pointer variable defines another variable. As a consequence, it is no longer possible to compile a list of a program's state just by looking at its source code. Not only the values of state variables but even their number can change over time.

As a final example, let us look at a high-level language with automatic memory management, Python. In Python, all data take the form of objects, which are referred to via their address in memory. A variable is a memory location that stores a memory address. Assigning a new value to the variable changes this memory address. Variables are thus part of the program's state. But objects can also store memory addresses of other objects. For example, a list is a sequence of memory locations, each of which stores the address of one list element. The state of a Python program consists of all references to all objects. If you want to compile a list of all these references, you have to start with the list of modules that is managed by the Python interpreter and recursively look at all references stored by the objects you encounter. Then you have to do another round with the local variables of all active functions and methods. The complexity of a Python program's state is also reflected in the many ways this state can be changed. Assignments to variables or list elements are the most obvious ones, but appending to a list also changes the state, as do many of the methods that Python proposes for its built-in data structures.

5.4.2 Stateless computing

The most extreme approach to avoiding state corruption stipulates that if humans are bad at managing the state of a computer, perhaps they should not do it at all. Can one write programs without ever changing the contents of a memory area? The answer is yes, and I have given an illustration in section 3.1. The term rewriting approach to computation that I have explained there uses no variables, nor any form of state modification. It can be shown that any computation can be expressed in the form of rewrite rules, and therefore state modification can clearly be avoided. A closer look at how we compute by hand confirms this: we write down expression after expression, but we never take an eraser in order to change an expression written down earlier.

Programming styles that do not rely on explicit state modifications are known as *functional programming*. It is called 'functional' because its program abstractions behave like mathematical functions: they compute result values from argument values without any other effect. If you re-read section 5.3.1 now, you will better understand why I recommended avoiding the use of global variables in procedures.

In spite of its age—the idea goes back to Alonzo Church's lambda calculus from the 1930s—and its advantages for ensuring the correctness of software, functional programming plays only a marginal role in computational science today. The main reason is that functional programming is not a good fit for today's computers. A processor instruction set is the very opposite of functional: most instructions explicitly change the contents of a memory location. Functional programs must therefore be translated to non-functional ones. This is not difficult in principle, but it is very difficult to obtain an efficient result. For a long time, functional programming was therefore considered too inefficient for use in real life. Compilers have improved and computers have become faster, with the result that functional programming slowly finds its way into many domains of computing, but scientific computing is not yet one of them.

5.4.3 State protection

If we do not want to take the big step towards functional programming, we have to live with programs that directly modify the contents of memory at some point. But we can still impose constraints on such modifications, to reduce the risk of mistakes. The main constraint type limits modifications to specific memory areas. On a modern computer, the processor itself performs checks to prevent a program from changing memory areas that do not belong to it, such as memory areas used by the operating system. Compilers can introduce other types of checks, preventing, for example, a program from changing element number five of an array having only three elements.

Automatic memory management with garbage collection, which I have mentioned in section 4.2.1, is another very effective protection mechanism. It eliminates mistakes in the handling of dynamically allocated memory, which are among the worst sources of hard-to-track-down problems. The reason for this is that with dynamic memory allocation, a single memory area is used for completely unrelated tasks in the course of program execution. It is not even the program that decides which memory area to reuse when, but the operating system. The result of a program modifying a memory region that no longer belongs to it can therefore change every time the program is run, causing apparently random erroneous behavior.

Object-oriented programming can also be considered a form of state protection. The data structures defined in a class can only be modified by methods from the same class. From the outside, the state of an object can thus only be modified by calling its methods. Clever design can allow much state manipulation inside a class for efficiency, but allow little or no state modification from the outside.

It is always a good idea to complement the state protection methods that I have summarized above by design rules in one's own programs. A good principle is to keep state modifications local to some procedure. A procedure may thus, for example, create a new list data structure and then add elements to it, but once such a list leaves the procedure in the form of a return value, it should not be modified any more. However, what matters more than the exact rules one adopts is clear documentation: the interface of every procedure should clearly state if it modifies stateful data it receives as input, e.g. a list passed to it as an argument.

5.5 Incidental complexity and technical debt

Software complexity is of course not a problem specific to computational science. It concerns all application domains of computing. It is thus not surprising that software complexity is a recurrent topic in software engineering. A distinction that has turned out to be useful in this context is the one between *essential* and *incidental* (also called *accidental*) complexity in software [11]. Essential complexity has its origin in the task that the software is supposed to accomplish. There is no way to reduce or remove it, except perhaps by discovering a revolutionary simpler approach to the whole problem. In computational science, common causes are complex scientific models. Incidental complexity comes from the computational tools that we use. We could in principle remove it completely, but for some reason we do not. When a piece of software becomes too complex for its developers or users to understand, it is worth looking for sources of incidental complexity because that is where improvements are possible.

The ultimate cause for incidental complexity is almost always an insufficient effort to do the best job possible. Most software in science is developed under resource constraints, and in particular under time pressure. We thus choose libraries and even programming languages that we are familiar with, even though they may not be the best choice for the task. We use algorithms and data structures we know, rather than search the literature for potentially better ones. After writing a first version of some code, we usually have a better understanding of the problem that would allow us to improve the original design, but we do not because the first draft is good enough to get the next paper out. And since almost everyone in the computing business reasons in the same way, we inherit much incidental complexity from others. Our computers, operating systems, compilers, editors, etc are more complex than they need to be, both individually and in the way they work together. Consider for a moment on which computing problems you spend most of your time. Is it thinking about scientific models and computational methods? Or is it installing software, converting data from one file format to another, and searching the Internet for ways to work around a bug in someone else's software?

A useful metaphor for thinking about these problems is *technical debt*, a concept that has recently become popular in the software industry. In analogy to a financial debt, a technical debt is a long-term obligation incurred in exchange for a short-term benefit. Keeping your first somewhat sloppy code design lets you produce publishable results earlier, but it will become an obstacle to future work. One day you will have to rewrite that code, if you want to continue to rely on it. The other option is, of course, defaulting on the debt: you stop using your code, or you accept doing bad science using code you do not really trust yourself any more.

The point of the technical debt metaphor is to make the trade-off between short and long term criteria explicit. When faced with a major decision, such as which languages or libraries to use, or whether to modify existing code or start from scratch, treat it as a contract with your future self and consider the technical debt incurred for each choice. Our natural tendency is to emphasize short-term costs and benefits over long-term ones, because the short-term aspects are much easier to evaluate. The main effort in technical debt analysis is therefore to concentrate on the future. Consider for how long you expect to be working on problems similar to the current one. Imagine the ideal starting conditions for your next project, and compare to what you expect to have at the end of the current one. Make a list of the technical problems that you had to deal with recently, and ask yourself if you might have to deal with them again, making it worthwhile to invest in a durable solution. As a general rule, an evaluation of technical debt points out the importance of infrastructure technology (everything not specifically made for a project) and acquiring new competences, which are otherwise often neglected.

5.6 Further reading

Most of the topics of this chapter are discussed in detail in many books written for software developers. Unfortunately, such books rarely address the particularities of computational science, such as the difficulties related to numerical computations. A good source for pedagogical articles written specifically for scientists is the IEEE magazine *Computing in Science and Engineering*.

The subject of errors in scientific software [1] is being discussed more and more as such problems are discovered. For examples from different domains, see [12, 13], and [14]. David Soergel [15] has provided a more theoretical discussion of the problem.

Another interesting case study is the 'war over supercooled water' [16], a seven-year long battle between two research groups that could only be resolved when the code underlying the conflicting simulations was shared. And yet, the cause was not a bug in the code, but a detail of the simulation protocol that was not documented outside of the code.

One of the rare books about verification and validation that does specifically deal with scientific computing is *Verification and Validation in Scientific Computing* by Oberkampf and Roy [17]. It discusses verification and validation both for scientific software and for the numerical methods that it implements.

There are support tools for software testing for all of today's popular programming languages. Some of them are actually part of the language's set of standard tools, others are distributed separately. They usually come with good documentation and a series of examples. The test suites that come with Open Source scientific software packages are also a good source for inspiration.

Abstractions are treated thoroughly in the first two chapters of *The Structure and Interpretation of Computer Programs* by Abelson and Sussman [18]. These two chapters use a functional programming style, to which chapter 3 adds a good discussion of mutable state in computer programs.

Herbert Simon's 1962 essay *The Architecture of Complexity* [4] remains a good introduction to the issues of taming complexity. It is also included in his book *The Sciences of the Artificial* [19].

References

[1] Merali Z 2010 Computational science: …Error *Nature* **467** 775–7

[2] Berry G *Pourquoi et comment le monde devient numérique* http://www.college-de-france.fr/site/gerard-berry/inaugural-lecture-2008-01-17-18h00.htm. Leçon inaugurale 2007-8, Collège de France

[3] Boldo S, Clément F, Filliâtre J-C, Mayero M, Melquiond G and Weis P 2014 Trusting computations: A mechanized proof from partial differential equations to actual program *Comput. Math. Appl.* **68** 325–52

[4] Simon H 1962 The architecture of complexity *Proc. Am. Philos. Soc.* **106** 467–82

[5] Norvig P *Teach Yourself Programming in Ten Years* http://norvig.com/21-days.html.

[6] The World Wide Web Consortium *Extensible Markup Language (XML)* http://www.w3.org/XML/.

[7] Crockford D *Introducing JSON* https://www.json.org/.

[8] Hall S R 1991 The STAR file: A new format for electronic data transfer and archiving *J. Chem. Inf. Comput. Sci.* **31** 326–33

[9] NASA *FITS–Flexible Image Transport System* https://fits.gsfc.nasa.gov/.

[10] The HDF Group *Hdf5* https://www.hdfgroup.org/HDF5/.

[11] Brooks F P J 1987 No silver bullet: essence and accidents of software engineering *Computer* **20** 10–9

[12] Gronenschild E H B M, Habets P, Jacobs H I L, Mengelers R, Rozendaal N, van Os J and Marcelis M 2012 The effects of FreeSurfer Version, workstation type, and Macintosh operating system version on anatomical volume and cortical thickness measurements *PLoS One* **7** e38234

[13] Flouri T, Kobert K, Rognes T and Stamatakis A 2015 Are all global alignment algorithms and implementations correct? bioRxiv 031500

[14] Neupane J B, Neupane R P, Luo Y, Yoshida W Y, Sun R and Williams P G 2019 Characterization of Leptazolines A–D, polar oxazolines from the Cyanobacterium *Leptolyngbya* sp., reveals a glitch with the 'Willoughby–Hoye' scripts for calculating NMR chemical shifts *Org. Lett.* **21** 8449–53

[15] Soergel D A W 2014 Rampant software errors undermine scientific results *F1000Research* **3** 303

[16] Smart A G 2018 The war over supercooled water *Physics Today* https://physicstoday.scitation.org/do/10.1063/PT.6.1.20180822a/full/

[17] Oberkampf W L and Roy C J 2010 *Verification and Validation in Scientific Computing* 1st edn (Cambridge: Cambridge University Press)

[18] Abelson H and Sussman G J 1996 *Structure and Interpretation of Computer Programs* 2nd edn (Cambridge, MA: MIT Press)

[19] Simon H 1996 *The Sciences of the Artificial* 3rd edn (Cambridge, MA: MIT Press)

Computation in Science (Second Edition)
From concepts to practice
Konrad Hinsen

Chapter 6

Computational reproducibility

One of the most disconcerting surprises in the scientific research of the early 21st century has been the observation that many published results, or conclusions drawn from results, could not be reproduced by other researchers. This so-called *reproducibility crisis* or *replication crisis* is the subject of an ongoing debate as I am writing this chapter. This debate is fueled by surprise, by fear for the reputation of science in the general public and among decision makers, but also by a lot of confusion as people from different scientific disciplines, in which reproducibility has historically played very different roles, try to figure out how serious the situation actually is and what can be done to improve everyone's research practices.

Of all the topics covered in this book, reproducibility is the least settled one. If you read this chapter a few years from now, you may well wonder what all the fuss was about. But even if you live in a world in which reproducibility is a problem of the past, it may be of interest to understand how it happened.

I will begin with an introduction to reproducibility in science in general (section 6.1) and to the often confusing terminology around it (section 6.2), in order to put computational reproducibility in the wider context of the scientific method. This will set the stage for the main part of this chapter, which explains the double role that computation has played in the origins of the reproducibility crisis (section 6.3) and the root causes of computational non-reproducibility (sections 6.4 and 6.5). These two sections emphasize an understanding of the problem and how it can be solved in principle, even though the existing practical solutions are only just beginning to move beyond the proof-of-concept stage. In section 6.8, I then start from the opposite end and outline steps that computational scientists can take immediately to improve the reproducibility of their work, even though they cannot reach the ultimate goal of complete long-term reproducibility.

6.1 Reproducibility: a core value of science

Reproducibility has been a key ingredient of the scientific method ever since its beginnings in the 17th century. One reason is that science aims for objective findings, findings that are accessible to anyone. If you claim to have spotted a flying saucer, but nobody else confirms that observation, then your claim does not count as scientific evidence. Another reason for insisting on reproducibility is quality control. Everybody makes mistakes, including scientists. Moreover, even the best scientists suffer from biases of various kinds. For example, they are more likely to look for confirmations of their hypotheses than for refutations. If several scientists independently make the same observation, the observation will be considered more reliable. Reproducibility has thus become an indicator of trustworthiness.

However, reproducibility has always been an ideal rather than the norm of real-life research. An early well-documented reproducibility dispute happened between Christiaan Huygens and Robert Boyle, both experimenting with air pumps in the 1660s [1]. In theory, experimental reproducibility is ensured by a thorough documentation of the experiment. In practice, any written documentation is likely to be incomplete because its author has no way of knowing what information someone else would require for reproduction. Scientists skim over details of their equipment that they consider irrelevant, and don't report facts that they take for granted or are not even aware of knowing, i.e. so-called *tacit knowledge*. The reproducibility status of scientific work thus remains uncertain until someone actually makes a reproduction attempt.

Reproducibility has become a complex subject because science has changed significantly since the 17th century. Early science was mostly basic astronomy, physics, and chemistry. Experiments were simple and usually doable by well-resourced individuals. Today, scientists sometimes study inherently non-repeatable or very hard to repeat events. Astronomers spotting a supernova don't expect to see it again in the future. Particle physicists at the Large Hadron Collider in Geneva know that there is no other equipment in the world where their experiments could be checked independently. Biologists working with animals are aware of their individuality and don't expect every animal to behave in the same way when exposed to the same conditions. Anthropologists studying people from a remote culture are aware of their own behavior having an impact on their subjects, and thus don't expect another anthropologist to make exactly the same observations. In such situations, reproducibility is not applicable, and other indicators of trustworthiness have to be used.

Another important change in scientific practice is that the processing steps that lie between raw observations, such as instrument readings, and findings that scientists and non-scientists are actually interested in, have steadily gotten more numerous and more complex. What we publish today as the result of a scientific study is usually *inferences* made on the basis of both observations and models that are assumed to hold (see also sections 2.3.1 and 2.3.2). Statistical inference has taken a particularly prominent place in many scientific disciplines. To answer a question such as 'does drug A improve the symptoms of illness B', it is not sufficient to make an observation. Instead, two groups of patients must be formed, which must be representative of illness B. One group receives drug A, whereas the other one doesn't. Differences in symptoms are then observed for each patient, and statistical inference methods are applied to these observations to decide if there is any systematic difference between the two groups that can be ascribed to drug A. In such situations, it is not obvious what reproducibility actually means. Is it the raw observations that are supposed to be reproducible, on the same groups of patients? Or is it the inferred findings that should be reproducible, even with differently chosen groups of patients? This is one reason why the debate about the reproducibility crisis is so rich in misunderstandings.

Reproducibility has thus evolved from a relatively simple must-have feature to one out of several quality indicators for scientific work, and moreover one that has to be appreciated in the context of the state of the art of each domain. It is always an ideal worth pursuing, but a failure to achieve it should not automatically be seen as a sign of a crisis in science, although sometimes it is.

6.2 Repeating, reproducing, replicating

The current debate around reproducibility issues is still in its early phase, and terminology has not yet stabilized. It is an unfortunate reality that different authors use the same terms with different, sometimes conflicting, meanings. The use of terms that I will explain in this section and follow in the rest of this chapter is, in my opinion, the currently dominant one in the discussion of computational reproducibility, but it might well evolve in the future.

A typical research study starts from a research question, to which answers are sought through some combination of observation and reasoning. Observations most commonly happen in the context of experiments, i.e. situations specifically created to permit an observation. Reasoning includes computation as a particularly important technique. Other researchers critically investigating this study may follow two basic approaches: they can try to *verify* the use of techniques and the reasoning in order to be sure that everything was done correctly, or they can try to *validate* the methods that were used in order to convince themselves that they are appropriate to answer the initial research question (see also section 5.2). This includes in particular checking for the *robustness* of the methods, i.e. exploring if minor variations in the protocol that are unrelated to the research question can nevertheless have an impact on the results.

My choice of terminology is to use 'reproducing', 'reproduction', and 'reproducibility' in the context of verification, whereas 'replicating', 'replication', and 'replicability' belong to the realm of validation.

Unfortunately, the distinction between verification and validation is not as clear-cut as it seems. Reproducing an experiment should consist of doing everything in exactly the same way: use the same samples, the same instruments, and ensure that every imaginable parameter of the environment (temperature, ambient light, ⋯) is the same as well. That is of course impossible in general: the reproducer doesn't usually have the required information (few scientific papers report ambient light levels), nor access to exactly the same instruments. But when you say 'let's forget about ambient light, it shouldn't matter', then you are assuming robustness, which is established as part of validation. You have made a first step away from reproduction towards replication. In experimental science, control over instruments and samples is always limited. Reproduction, and more generally verification, are therefore limited in scope as well.

For reasoning, and in particular computation, the situation is different. Verification consists of going through the steps one by one and comparing results. Validation consists of questioning technical choices that are unrelated to the research question. For example, if a line of reasoning requires the numerical solution of a differential equation, a technically necessary but (ideally) scientifically irrelevant choice is the choice of an integration algorithm and its parameters (step size etc, see section 2.1.2). A validation attempt could thus use a different algorithm, and compare the final results. The distinction between verification and validation is clearer for reasoning, because there are in principle no unknowns. The author of an article usually omits some details of the reasoning for brevity, assuming that every interested reader will be familiar with the techniques of the domain. This assumption may turn out to be wrong, but then the verifying reader will notice this lack of information. The reviewer of an article submitted to a journal can even request the author to supply the missing details. Verification is therefore a much more powerful technique for reasoning than it is for observations.

Since a typical scientific study combines observations and reasoning, there are many possible combinations of verification and validation of the individual parts. It is thus not obvious what 'reproducing' or 'replicating' an entire study would mean. Various authors have introduced additional terms, such as 'repeating' (an experiment or a computation), 're-running' (a program), or 'reusing' (a method or a piece of software), but there isn't much consensus about their meaning. I will therefore only use the two basic terms that I have defined above, and apply them to well-defined steps of scientific work.

6.3 The role of computation in the reproducibility crisis

In the context of today's scientific research, it is helpful to distinguish between three categories of reproducibility issues:

- **Experimental reproducibility** refers to the outcomes of observations. Can someone else create a similar experimental setup, and then make observations that are close enough to the original ones?
- **Statistical reproducibility** refers to the outcomes of statistical inferences from observations made on samples of subjects, be they electrons, cells, or people. Can someone else perform a similar experiment, necessarily on a different sample, and infer similar results as the original study?
- **Computational reproducibility** refers to the results of non-trivial computations. Can someone else perform the same computation on the same input data and obtain the same results?

These categories do not cover every possible situation. For example, the reproducibility of scientific reasoning presented in plain language does not fall into any of these categories. However, as far as the current debate about the reproducibility crisis is concerned, these three kinds of reproducibility are all that matters.

It is interesting to note that among the examples commonly cited as evidence for the reproducibility crisis, none is related to experimental reproducibility[1]. This is not because experimental reproducibility is no longer an issue, quite the contrary. However, experimental reproducibility is a well-understood issue in most scientific disciplines, one that researchers deal with as part of their routine work of doing experiments and reviewing the work of others. Only rare cases of non-reproducibility ever come to the attention of a wider public, an example being the 'cold fusion' debate in the 1990s, which is nicely explained in Wikipedia. The debate about the reproducibility crisis has been fueled by examples of statistical and computational non-reproducibility, both of which are recent phenomena that took the scientific community by surprise.

Nevertheless, experimental reproducibility is important in the debate, because so many people refer to it. Often it is just a historical reference, pointing out the fundamental role of reproducibility in the development of the scientific method. But many people fail to distinguish between experimental and statistical reproducibility, because statistical inference is based on experimental input and its results are often presented as the outcome of an experiment. Others fail to see the difference between experiments and reasoning in the applicability of verification techniques, and argue as if computations were experiments.

Not only are statistical and computational (ir-)reproducibility recent phenomena, they are also phenomena introduced by computational methods. While this is evident for computational reproducibility, it requires some explanation for statistical inference. Statistical inference techniques have been developed since the 1920s, starting with the seminal work by Ronald Fisher. However, before the widespread availability of computers, the only way to apply statistical inference in research was through collaboration with trained statisticians. It is software that has made statistical methods available as black-box tools that can be deployed easily with a few mouse clicks (see section 7.2 for a further discussion). Moreover, nothing in the software or its documentation warns potential users about the importance of properly understanding the conditions under which the methods can be safely applied. Statistical irreproducibility is most often the consequence of incorrect or inappropriate use of statistical inference.

6.4 Non-reproducible determinism

The very existence of computational irreproducibility is difficult to envisage for many scientists. Arithmetic looks like the most certain of all things. Two plus two is four, as it was a thousand years ago and will be a thousand years in the future. Sure,

---

[1] There are a few cases of fraud that led to non-reproducible experimental findings, but fraud is not the central issue of the reproducibility crisis.

the computations that computers do for us are a lot more complicated, but it's still just a well-defined chain of deterministic operations[2]. So maybe it's the hardware that isn't reliable? Maybe it makes a mistake in an operation every now and then? Or memory gets corrupted? This is indeed potentially a problem for long-running large-memory jobs on supercomputers, but the typical data analysis you run in a few minutes on your laptop is not affected by hardware mistakes. The best evidence is empirical: if you re-run the same program a few times in a row, you do get the same results.

The last observation is also the key to the explanation of the reproducibility paradox. If you re-run the same program a few times in a row, you get the same results. When you don't get the same results, it's because you are using a different computer, or the same computer a long time later. What's different then is the *software environment* that the computer provides. You are not really running the same computation, it only *seems* to be the same computation because all the software you care about is the same, or at least almost the same—a small increase in the version number shouldn't matter, right?

If you have read section 6.2 carefully, you will recognize the phrase 'shouldn't matter'—that's testing for robustness, i.e. validation, not verification. For testing reproducibility, you need the *same* software, not just *almost the same* software—whatever that may actually mean, as there is no similarity measure for software. If software developers increase the version number, they signal that something has changed. Whether or not that change affects *your* computation is something that only you can figure out, and only by actually re-running your computation and comparing the results. That's a test for robustness, which is a useful test to do from time to time, but it's not a test for reproducibility.

Unfortunately, re-running the exact same software is easier said than done. The software packages that you are aware of are just the tip of an iceberg. They rely on a mostly invisible foundation that consists of a large number of software packages whose names you are probably not familiar with.

Figure 6.1 shows an example of the run-time dependency graph of a piece of scientific software. We will see later that there are several types of dependencies. Run-time dependencies are those that you need to have on your computer in order to run the software, in addition to the basic operating system software which is usually not included in a dependency graph for simplicity. I have chosen the example, OpenBabel, for the small size of its dependency graph, which makes it fit into this book. For many popular scientific software packages, the dependency graphs are much larger. For larger examples, and an explanation of how these graphs have been obtained, see the companion Web site.

In principle, every piece of software in the run-time dependency graph of your computation can have an impact on your results. Any change, intentional or accidental, can make your results non-reproducible. In practice, for any one given

---

[2] There is an important exception: some parallel computing techniques are not deterministic, and therefore not reproducible (see section 4.1.4). However, only a small fraction of computations in science are concerned by this.

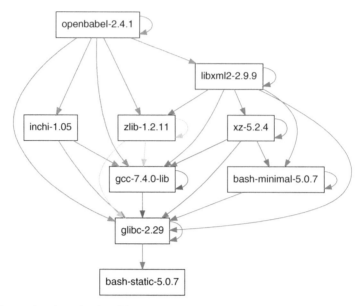

Figure 6.1. The run-time dependencies of OpenBabel, a data conversion toolkit for chemistry. Each box stands for the files belonging to a software package. Arrows indicate file-level dependencies. Arrows pointing to the same box thus indicate dependencies between files in the same package.

execution of a program, many dependencies don't matter, but it is nearly impossible to find out which ones. In the example of figure 6.1, knowing that OpenBabel does file format conversions, it seems safe to assume that libxml2 will have no impact unless one of the file formats in a conversion process is based on XML, but such educated guesses can go wrong. It is best to assume that all software in the dependency graph can have an impact on a computation's result.

Reproducing a result therefore involves re-running exactly the same software. And that in turn requires at the very least *knowing* all the software packages that appear in the run-time dependency graph, with their version numbers. Next, it requires being able to *re-create this software assembly* at a later time, or on a different computer. Computational reproducibility is thus a matter of good software management practices. Good software management practices depend to a large degree on good support tools for managing reproducible software. Such tools have been under development for a few years. They are still too complicated to use for most computational scientists, but I would like to encourage everyone with some technical interest to have a look at them. The dependency graphs in this chapter, and on the companion Web site, have been generated using one such tool, GNU Guix, and the Web site provides more information about how this was done. The other management tool for fully reproducible software, and in fact historically the first one, is Nix. Nix and Guix apply the same principles, but differ in many implementation choices.

In the next section, I will outline the challenges and trade-offs that management tools for reproducibility have to deal with, which should also make clear why most proposed solutions for ensuring computational reproducibility fall short of their goal. This is the most technical section of this chapter, so you may prefer to skip it at first reading and return to it later.

6.5 Staged computation

In the last section, I have explained that the hard problem in ensuring computational reproducibility is keeping track of all the software involved. In figure 6.1, I have shown an example of a dependency graph, which describes the software assembly that needs to be reproduced in order to reproduce any result obtained by running it. And I suspect that some readers have shrugged this off as no more than an unpleasant chore. Installing nine software packages cannot be so hard! But remember that my example was chosen for the simplicity of its dependency graph. Other software is likely to require the installation of more than nine packages. However, there is a much bigger obstacle on the road to reproducible computing.

Each node in a run-time dependency graph represents a software package that must be present on a computer's file system. In practice, that's one directory for each package, containing multiple files. The files are what the computer needs to run the software, and that includes what programmers call the program's *binaries* (see the explanation of compilation in section 4.2), i.e. files containing sequences of processor instructions (see section 4.1.2). What software developers produce, distribute, and archive (e.g. on the Software Heritage archive [2]) is not binaries, but the source code from which binaries are produced by compilation. So if you want to re-create an identical assembly of binaries, at a later time or on a different computer, you have two options: preserve and restore the binaries, or recompile the source code that others already preserve for you. Before discussing the trade-offs involved in this choice, I will explain the challenges that either option presents.

6.5.1 Preserving compiled code

At first sight, preserving and restoring the compiled binaries looks like an easy task. They are just files, after all, so all it takes is keeping a copy in a safe place. When you need them again, you copy them back to where they were initially. There are some obvious issues with access rights, so perhaps only a computer's administrator could do it, depending on how things are arranged, but these are well-understood issues to which solutions can be found.

The real obstacle is something else: the architecture of today's operating systems for desktop computers, which goes back to the 1970s, is based on the principle that each computer holds a single software environment, shared by all of its users. Moreover, the only operations for managing this environment are installing new software, and updating existing software. These choices were very reasonable at a time when memory and disk space were expensive, and the optimistic expectation that software only gets better with time had not yet been dampened by reality. Given this single-environment architecture, what is likely to happen when you want to copy your archived binaries back to their original place is a conflict: newer versions of some software packages have taken the place of those you wish to restore, and some other software on your computer depends on these new versions. If you insist, you will likely break your software environment.

When it became evident that managing software environments was likely to lead to conflicts in a single-environment architecture, various initiatives were launched to create more or less isolated sub-environments that could be transferred from one computer to another. The different approaches vary in how solidly these sub-environments are isolated from each other, and in how general they are in accommodating diverse pieces of software. One extreme approach is the *virtual machine*, which is a computer on its own that is simulated on another computer. By default, such a virtual machine shares no data with its host. This perfect isolation comes at a cost in terms of storage size, as even a minimal virtual machine weighs in at hundreds of megabytes. The other main cost is inconvenience of use, in particular when several virtual machines must be made to work together. At the other end of the scale, there are lightweight approaches such as the virtual environments of the Python language, which are directories in the file system populated with links to the 'real' files. There is little overhead in using such environments, but they are limited to software written in Python, tend to be brittle, and cannot be transferred easily to another computer. Today, the most popular approach is the *container*, which is about halfway between the two extremes outlined above. Like a virtual environment, a container is basically a directory in the file system, but this directory is presented to the software running in the container as if it were the complete environment, much like the simulated disks of a virtual machine. Contrary to a virtual machine, containers share the basic operating system with its host, which makes them smaller and more efficient, but also makes it easier to share data between multiple containers.

These recent support technologies make it possible to transfer and archive software environments that include binaries. However, its convenience comes at a price. I have already mentioned the most visible one: increased size. A less obvious one could turn out to be more problematic in the long run: the software implementing the support technology becomes an additional dependency. As I mentioned above, operating system software is usually not included in the dependency graph, but it is nevertheless a requirement to run anything at all. With containers, for example, the container management software must be added to the basic operating system. And since containers, unlike operating systems, are recent technology (invented in the 2010s rather than the 1970s), it is hard to foresee if they will still be around, and compatible with today's versions, a few decades from now.

6.5.2 Reproducible builds

Recompiling source code also looks like an easy task at first sight. If it has been done once, it can be done again. But then, everything about computational reproducibility looks easy at first sight. The devil is in the details.

Compiling source code into binaries is, as I pointed out in section 4.2, just another computation. A program (the compiler) transforms input data (the source code plus any compilation options) into output data (the binaries). This is fundamentally no

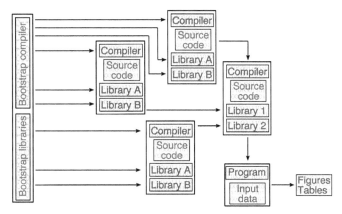

Figure 6.2. A much simplified staged computation, whose final result (bottom right) is figures and tables for inclusion in a journal article. Items shown in blue are human input, i.e. mainly source code. Items shown in magenta are data obtained from scientific instruments. Items shown in green are the output of a computation. On the left, the hand-coded binaries called the bootstrap seed.

different from OpenBabel reading a molecule description in one file format and converting it to another file format. But this also means that the reproducibility issues are exactly the same. If you want to get the exact same binaries, you will have to use the exact same input source code, and the exact same compiler options. The reproducibility of binaries, and thus of software environments, is exactly the same problem as the reproducibility of scientific computations. This doesn't sound good. Remember that we got interested in reproducible binaries as a way to solve the problem of reproducible results. But we ran into the same problem again. So did we really make progress?

The good news is yes, we did. Software has something of a chicken-or-egg problem: you need source code to produce binaries through compilation, but you also need the binaries for some other software (the compiler) for that step. Like for the chicken-or-egg question, the solution is to take a step back and look at how the *process* of software-compiling-other-software can be initiated. We started with a simple computation, such as converting a data file from one format to another. Then we added a step before that, which is compiling the conversion software's source code into binaries. Such a sequence, in which each step produces the *code* (rather than, say, the input data) of the subsequent step, is called a *staged computation*[3]. So we can reformulate our mission as making a staged computation reproducible. As we will see shortly, our staged computation is actually more complex than it seems to be so far. But framing it as a single staged computation, no matter how complex, provides the key to designing its reproducibility (figure 6.2).

In the above description, I have referred to compilers because they are the best known software tools that intervene in preparing source code execution, but there are others. The task of combining multiple binaries into a single one for execution by

---

[3] It is almost surprising that there is a specific term for this. After all, my example of data conversion is a rather typical computation. Almost all computations are staged computations.

the processor is traditionally handled by a *linker*. Before compilation, code is sometimes passed through a *pre-processor* for various reasons. The orchestration of all the steps involved in compiling and linking software has become a complex enough task to motivate the development of special tools (such as make, CMake, or Maven) that need to be taken into account as well. The complete process of creating the run-time files for a software package from its source code is called *building* the package, and all the tools that participate in this endeavor are collectively called *build tools*. A more precise description of our staged computation is thus that it consists of a build step followed by an execution step. For the example of file format conversion using OpenBabel, the build step builds the nine packages in figure 6.1, and the execution step does the conversion.

Build tools are, of course, nothing but yet more software packages. They exist as binary files on our computer, and those binary files must be built from source code. So we have one more step before the build step—the build step for the build tools of the ultimate build step. But that means more build tools that must be built. It looks like our staged computation will become an infinite sequence of steps! But that is, of course, impossible. An infinite sequence would take an infinite amount of time. You do have the software on your computer, which proves that its preparation was a finite process. The reason is that as you move along the build step chain towards its origins, you will find more and more packages requiring exactly the same build tools, and in particular a C compiler. In such a 'back to the roots' analysis, you will also find, at some point in the remote past, some pieces of software that were written directly in terms of processor instructions. In other words, hand-written binaries, which require no build step.

Most probably, those original hand-written binaries are nowhere to be found on your computer. People did write binaries by hand in the 1970s, for lack of choice, but hardly anyone does so today. The run-time packages that you have on your computer were most likely built on another computer. Our staged computation spans many computers over several decades! And that also means that making it fully reproducible, starting from hand-written code, is impossible, since the first software in the chain has been lost together with the computer it ran on. The best we can do is rebuild as much we can, starting from a minimal set of archived precompiled binaries, which typically include a small compiler. For an example of such a minimal starting point, see the GNU Mes project.

At this point, I can introduce a second type of dependency graph: the graph of recursive build dependencies. 'Build dependencies' means everything required to build the run-time form of a package. And 'recursive' means that it covers the full staged computation, including the build tools required to build all the other build tools. It's the most comprehensive kind of dependency graph, containing everything that can potentially have an impact on the results of a computation, with the sole exception of the basic operating system.

Unfortunately, the recursive build dependency graph for OpenBabel is already too large to fit on a page of this book, containing 121 packages with 2209 dependency relations between them. You can find it on the the companion Web site for this book, together with a few other examples of run-time and recursive build dependency graphs. The size of these graphs means that the only way to manage reproducible builds in practice is by automation. This is exactly what the software management tools Guix and Nix do (see section 6.4). Their key input is a manually curated database that lists the build dependencies for each package, and also stores the recipe for building each package from these dependencies. With this information, every software package can be re-built from its source code at any time, assuming (1) the continued availability of all the source code, (2) the continued availability of the operating system infrastructure required by the software management system itself, and (3) the continued existence of computers that can run this operating system infrastructure.

6.5.3 Preserving or rebuilding?

Now that we have seen the two main approaches to guaranteeing software reproducibility, which one is better? Given that I explained both in detail, it shouldn't come as a surprise that there is no clear winner. But the answer isn't even 'it depends', but rather 'we need both'.

Let's first consider a hypothetical 'rebuild only' approach. Every time you run OpenBabel for converting the description of a molecule to another format, which by itself typically takes less than second, you would have to wait for a monstrous sequence of build steps to complete. You would watch your computer download and build 121 software packages, of which at least one, the GNU Compiler Collection (gcc) is huge and requires half an hour of compilation on its own. This is clearly impractical, and that's why this approach has, to the best of my knowledge, never been attempted.

The 'archive only' approach, in contrast, is being actively promoted at this time as a solution to computational reproducibility. The software management systems most often cited in this context are the package manager conda and the container platform Docker. Both focus on binaries as the form of software to be distributed and re-used. They make it straightforward to formulate instructions of the form 'run the following command to obtain the software that was used in this study', and thus facilitate downloading and re-running software. One obvious problem is that the longevity of these instructions is questionable, since the archives commonly associated with conda or Docker are not backed up by any long-term commitment to software preservation. But there is a much more fundamental issue with reproducibility based on archived binaries.

In fact, what's the problem with non-reproducible computational results? They cannot be verified in any way. The existence of an electronic dataset proves no more than the existence of some software that can produce this particular sequence of bytes. It does not permit any scientific judgment about the dataset. Now suppose someone gives you archived binaries that produce this precise dataset. You have gained very little: before you knew that this software must exist, now you have it, but you still cannot check in detail what it does. Scientific judgment requires access to the only understandable representation of software, which is source code. But it isn't sufficient either to get the archived binaries plus the source code, even if it's the source code of everything in the recursive build dependency graph. If you cannot rebuild the binaries from the source code, then you have no reason to believe that the two are actually two different representations of the same software. Given the complexity of today's software builds, it's actually a safe bet to assume they are not, unless there is some evidence to the contrary.

To be fair to the proponents of archive-only software management tools, they usually do not propose an archive-only approach. They do advocate publishing the top-level code, usually a notebook, script, or workflow (see section 4.2.1), with the software management tool of their choice providing the environment in which this top-level code runs. In that case, readers do get some scientifically relevant information about the computations that were performed, and they can play with parameters, or plug in their own input data. But the criticism formulated in the last paragraph still applies for any deeper understanding or verification.

The only way to get practically usable software that is at the same time fully inspectable is a combination of the 'archive' and 'rebuild' approaches. This can be realized in different ways. An 'archive first' approach proposes a downloadable ready-to-run environment, but also supplies a recipe for rebuilding this environment from source code. A 'source code first' approach, such as taken by Guix and Nix, lets users define environments in terms of source code packages, but provides a cache of pre-built versions for the most commonly requested software, in order to avoid needless rebuilding. The key requirement is that anyone can at any time verify the correspondence between the source code and the binaries built from it, by launching an automated procedure. This possibility acts as a double source of trust: the automated build procedure ensures the absence of operator mistakes, and the ability for anyone to re-run it provides evidence for the absence of evil-minded manipulation.

6.6 Replicability, robustness, and reuse

The last two sections have shown that computational reproducibility, as defined in section 6.2, is a technically challenging subject. I hope to have made clear that this is mainly an issue of insufficient tool support. The underlying issues are well understood, and reproducibility can be assured by software tools, even though at this time the few such tools we have do not cover everybody's needs. Without good tools, ensuring perfect reproducibility requires an effort that most computational scientists rightly consider unreasonable, because it comes down to asking humans to do the work of a computer. This is why many researchers argue that some imperfect form of reproducibility, mainly aimed at providing reviewers and early readers of a scientific paper with the means to evaluate the computational aspects, is sufficient, and that long-term efforts should concentrate on replicability rather than reproducibility.

According to the definition I have adopted (section 6.2), replicability testing is a form of validation, aiming at evaluating the suitability of a computational technique for answering specific scientific questions. A particularly important aspect in computational practice is evaluating a method's robustness to changes in irrelevant technical details. The reason for this is the presence of chaos in computation (see section 5.1), which makes robustness very difficult to achieve by design, leaving no other possibility than to evaluate it regularly and fix problems as they become apparent. Robustness matters because a computer program that produces numbers in agreement with experiment only when compiled using a particular version of a particular compiler is suspect, as compiler details should not enter into a scientific model. More generally, no specific aspect of the implementation of a model or method in terms of software should matter for science[4]. At the extreme, it should be possible to start from scratch, writing completely new software based on nothing but the description of models and methods in scientific publications (see section 5.2.2), and get results that lead to the same scientific conclusions.

While it is certainly true that replicability testing is important, it is not a replacement for ensuring reproducibility. The two notions are complementary, because judging replicability is very difficult in the absence of reproducibility. Consider the following situation: Alice and Bob both explore if the results of a published computational notebook depend on the version of a library being used. Alice finds a small difference in results between versions 1 and 2 of the library, Bob says they are exactly the same. If Alice's and Bob's tests are reproducible, they can look at each other's work and reach an agreement. There are four possible outcomes: Alice has made a mistake, Bob has made a mistake, both of them have made mistakes, or there is some other, so far unsuspected, difference between their computations that is responsible for the change in the result. But if Alice's and Bob's tests are not reproducible, meaning that Alice's computation doesn't work on Bob's computer and vice versa, there is nothing to be done. There is obviously *some* difference, but nobody can figure out what it is because some details of the computations are unknown.

Whereas the importance of robustness is generally recognized, best practices for evaluating robustness and reporting on it remain to be developed. A major problem is that there are so many parameters that can potentially be varied: the versions of all software packages in the computation's recursive build dependency graph, plus all compilation and configuration options. Most robustness tests focus on the practically most relevant change: updating software packages to newer versions. The only parameter being varied is time: the computation is re-run from time to time, substituting the currently most recent version of each software package, and the results are compared to those obtained earlier. This form of testing (see section 5.2.3) is known as *continuous integration testing*. It is a technique imported from software engineering, where it is usually applied at a fine-grained level in the course of software development: every time the software source code is changed, its test suite is executed again.

An important reason for ensuring and testing robustness is *reuse*, another concept often confounded with reproducibility and replicability. Reuse consists of applying research software, with or without adaptations, to the study of somewhat different

---

[4] Unless, of course, the software itself is the subject of scientific study.

scientific questions. This can be done by the authors of the software, but also by someone else. Reproducibility of the original work, and evidence for robustness of the software, are both important elements of trust in the suitability of scientific software for future work.

In addition to robustness testing, there are many more opportunities for replicability checks that are just beginning to be exploited. Popular scientific models and methods have often been implemented several times in software, either because different teams had different technical requirements, or because they were unaware of each other's work, or unable to access it. It is also common for a scientist to re-implement an interesting method found in the literature in order to acquire a better understanding of how it works. A careful comparison of such multiple implementations, applied to the same scientific problem, can help other scientists choose trustworthy software to base their work on.

6.7 Managing software evolution

In the last section, I mentioned continuous integration testing as a technique for evaluating a particularly important aspect of robustness: the sensitivity of computational results to changes in the software's dependencies. However, continuous integration testing merely detects robustness issues. The question of how to deal with disruptive changes is a much more difficult one. Software collapse, i.e. the failure of software as a consequence of changes in the foundations that it is built on (figure 6.3), has become a routine event in many scientists' lives. The choice of an appropriate strategy depends on many factors, of which the two most important ones are the weight of software development in one's own work, and the time scale of methodological change in one's domain of research.

Dependencies are a novel phenomenon in scientific research that is due to the continuous growth in complexity of scientific software (see chapter 5). Scientists have always 'seen a little further by standing on the shoulders of giants', as Isaac Newton famously wrote to Robert Hooke in 1676. All new research builds on earlier work of many others. But it is the ideas and insights of earlier work that scientists used to build on, not its concrete expression on printed paper, or the experimental equipment used by their predecessors. Early computational science proceeded in the same way, with scientists taking up ideas from others but re-implementing them in

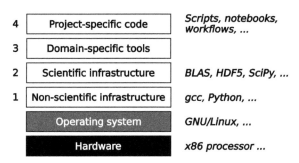

Figure 6.3. A typical scientific software stack, in which each layer depends on the layers below it.

their own software, or adapting someone else's software after a detailed study of the code. Donald Knuth made the distinction between 'reusable' and 're-editable' software [3], using the latter term to refer to this traditional approach of intellectually owning the software one uses:

> I also must confess to a strong bias against the fashion for reusable code. To me, 're-editable code' is much, much better than an untouchable black box or toolkit. I could go on and on about this. If you're totally convinced that reusable code is wonderful, I probably won't be able to sway you anyway, but youll never convince me that reusable code isn't mostly a menace.

In computational science, statistical irreproducibility (see section 6.3) and software collapse are two expressions of the menace that Knuth refers to.

However, computational science has so far followed the practices of the software industry, whose dogma promotes software building blocks that are produced by experts for a wide range of potential clients. These clients interact with the software via an interface that hides most of the software's internals. The lower layers of figure 6.3 have been designed according to this dogma, with only the top layer, project-specific software, being treated as re-editable.

Unfortunately, the dogma of the software industry does not go well with the social and institutional structure of scientific research. Scientists produce software much like they do research: each team does whatever it likes, and then makes the outcome publicly available. Whereas commercial entities tend to sign contracts with their suppliers that define the rights and obligations of each party, computational scientists have to depend on software made by other teams, on whose evolution they have little influence. It doesn't help that the architecture of today's operating systems (see section 6.5) refer to software building blocks via names that have to be unique, preventing in particular the installation of two versions of the same component. This creates a strong coupling between otherwise unrelated pieces of software that is colloquially referred to as 'dependency hell': if both A and B depend on C, then updating A may require updating C, which in turn may cause B to collapse. Scientists thus have neither technical nor social means to protect their software effectively against collapse.

One strategy that many scientists choose, in particular if computation is not the most important tool in their daily work, is to avoid updating software. Never change a running system. Buy a computer, install the current versions of everything you need, and then use it without changes. There are two important caveats to this principle. First of all, your computer can break down, forcing you to move on to a new one. It may well be difficult or impossible to install an identical software stack on a new machine, as you have learned earlier in this chapter. One insurance against future trouble is to use only stable and Open Source software. Debian Linux, for example, provides an archive of its historical installation media, going back to release 3.0 from 2002. Another option is to install all software relevant to your research in a virtual machine, and keep backups of it. Better yet, combine both techniques, and add a Docker container image for convenience. The more options you leave your future self to rebuild your software stack, the better are your chances to succeed. The second caveat is cybersecurity. Security-critical bugs are found quite regularly in many widely used software packages. They are fixed in updates that you really need to apply if you don't want run into trouble. One solution is, again, to keep your research software in a virtual machine or a container, and regularly update your computer's main software installation. Unlike operating systems and Web browsers, research software rarely presents security risks, so it is usually safe to keep running old versions, but it's still a good idea to check the news from your favorite software projects to avoid bad surprises.

For most computational scientists, such a radical version freezing approach is not feasible. Those working in a field where methodological progress is rapid will want to get regular software updates for new features, and that means accepting breaking changes as well. Those collaborating with colleagues on a computational project have to synchronize software versions within the team. Finally, those who actively contribute to rapidly evolving scientific software obviously need to keep up with its changes in their own applications. Most computational scientists thus have to develop a strategy for dealing with software collapse.

The core of such a strategy is an evaluation of the rate of evolution and the rate of breaking changes in all relevant software packages. The two are not the same: software can evolve without breaking changes, if its authors make backwards compatibility a high priority. Software collapse becomes a problem if the rate of evolution of your own software, including your project-specific scripts and work-flows, is slower than the rate of breaking changes in any of your dependencies. In that situation, you adopt a user's point of view of your own code, and consider it a reliable tool for your research work. Collapse can then do a lot of damage. If your own code changes constantly as well, you remain in a state of vigilance, which includes for example running tests regularly. Disruptive changes in the foundations are then detected rapidly and can be dealt with efficiently.

The direct dependencies of a piece of software present the highest risk of collapse in practice, but in principle any package in the recursive build dependency graph (see section 6.5) can be a cause of trouble. A recent example is the end-of-support for the Python 2 language in early 2020, which came as an unpleasant surprise to many users of software written in Python 2 who were nevertheless barely aware of its existence. Likewise, each time Microsoft ends support for a version of its Windows operating system, some highly specialized scientific software collapses, often because device drivers for lab equipment don't work with later versions. Intentional disruptive changes in infrastructure software (levels 1 and 2 in figure 6.3) are fortunately rare, but they also cause a lot of damage.

The most difficult aspect in developing a strategy for avoiding software collapse is evaluating the rate of breaking changes in one's direct and indirect dependencies. Few development teams make explicit statements about the priority they place on avoiding breaking changes. The best indicator for stability is a written specification for which multiple implementations exist. This is the case for the main programming languages of the 20th century, such as Fortran, COBOL, C, C++, Common Lisp, or Java, but also of the standards defined by the World Wide Web Consortium [4] and other industry standards such as OpenGL. In the absence of standards, a project's adoption of the semantic versioning conventions [5] is a promising sign, because it shows that its maintainers are aware of software collapse issues. Moreover, the project's version number trajectory provides a good basis for evaluating its past rate of breaking changes.

Extrapolating a project's past rate of change to the future is, however, another source of risk. For scientific software in particular, the development teams themselves are often unstable, often relying on short-term and part-time collaborators such as thesis students and postdocs. As an example, the scientific Python ecosystem whose evolution started in 1995 with the 'Numerical Python' package was very stable during its first ten years, but then gradually transitioned into a fragile foundation following its massive adoption by the machine learning and data science communities. People from these young domains had no established software that they needed to protect from collapse, and technical priorities somewhat different from the domains that had previously dominated the ecosystem. As a consequence, much scientific Python software from the 1990s and 2000s has collapsed by now.

6.8 Best practices for reproducible and replicable computational science

In the preceding sections, I have explained the challenges involved in making computations reproducible, conclusions replicable, and scientific software robust and reusable. Unfortunately, it is easy to conclude that reproducibility remains an unrealistic goal for most scientists. While this is true when the highest reproducibility standards are applied, reproducibility is not an all or nothing affair. In the following, I will outline the steps that computational scientists can take today in order to improve the reproducibility of their work. In most cases, they will ensure that scientists with a similar background can reproduce the results up to a few months later.

Archive your code and input data. This may sounds trivial compared to the technical challenges discussed before, but the loss of code or data is in practice one of the most frequent obstacles to reproducibility. Note also that backups are not archives. An archive is actively managed to ensure the preservation of information over longer time spans, even beyond the typical lifetime of storage media. Moreover, an archive assigns a unique handle to each deposit that permits later retrieval. Today, there are high-quality public archives for research data and code, e.g. Zenodo and Software Heritage. Use them, or check with your research institution's librarian for other options that may be available to you.

Document the steps required to reproduce your results. Prepare instructions that start from a freshly configured computer (real or virtual) and explain step by step what needs to be done to obtain the figures in your latest publication. Follow your own instructions to recompute your results on a different computer (real or virtual). With experience, you may not need to do this every time, but it is very important initially to understand the level of detail required in your instructions.

Check your instructions for non-reproducible steps, and try to eliminate them. The most frequent non-reproducible step is downloading files from the Internet that may change over time. Whenever your instructions say 'download software package XXX', make sure you add a version number. As I have explained earlier, it is currently very difficult to do this down to the last detail, but every additional effort increases reproducibility, even if perfection cannot be attained. Prefer downloading from archives, using unambiguous handles such as DOIs, Software Heritage IDs, or git commit hashes, as opposed to downloading from mere repositories that keep files only for a limited length of time.

Pair up with a colleague for a reciprocal reproducibility check. The idea is simple: each partner applies the other's instructions and checks if they lead to the correct results. That takes some time, but it is not only a useful service to the partner and to the scientific community at large, but also a great learning experience to improve one's own reproducibility skills.

If your reproducibility instructions end up being long or complicated, and you wish to make your work more easily accessible to your colleagues, you can in addition prepare and publish easy to install binaries. These can take the form of a container image, or of packages for one of the numerous software package managers in existence. Remember, however, that container images and precompiled binaries are not a substitute for full installation instructions because they are in general not reproducible and their lifetime is uncertain (see section 6.5.3).

6.9 Further reading

The review article 'Making scientific computations reproducible' [6] summarizes the early efforts of geophysicist Jon Claerbout, who pioneered computational reproducibility in science. The level of reproducibility they achieved in 2000 remains difficult to attain for most computational scientists 20 years later. There are also useful reviews of the state of the art in computational fluid dynamics [7] and electronic structure calculations [8], and an interesting case study on the reproducibility of parallel computations [9].

The article 'What is replication?' [10] provides a careful definition of this concept. It focuses on experimental research, but its ideas are transferable to computation and very close to my definition in section 6.2.

Computational reproducibility also matters outside of scientific computing, wherever it is important to establish trust in software. This was first emphasized by Ken Thompson in his 1984 Turing Award lecture [11]. The 'Reproducible Builds' initiative [12] works towards improving the reproducibility of software binaries in general (see section 6.5).

The on-line journal *ReScience* [13, 14] is dedicated to reproducible replications of computational studies in all domains of research. Its articles can be seen as case studies for the problems of reproducibility and replicability.

References

[1] Shapin S and Schaffer S 1985 *Leviathan and the Air-Pump* (Princeton, NJ: Princeton University Press)

[2] Abramatic J-F, Di Cosmo R and Zacchiroli S 2018 Building the universal archive of source code *Commun. ACM* **61** 29–31

[3] Knuth D E and Binstock A 2008 *InformIT: interview with Donald Knuth* https://web.archive.org/web/20101203111941/ https://www.informit.com/articles/article.aspx?p=1193856

[4] Word Wide Web Consortium 2019 *W3C Standards* https://www.w3.org/standards/

[5] Preston-Werner T 2013 *Semantic Versioning 2.0.0* https://semver.org/

[6] Schwab M, Karrenbach N and Claerbout J 2000 Making scientific computations reproducible *Comput. Sci. Eng.* **2** 61–7

[7] Mesnard O and Barba L A 2017 Reproducible and replicable computational fluid dynamics: it's harder than you think *Comput. Sci. Eng.* **19** 44–55

[8] Lejaeghere K *et al* 2016 Reproducibility in density functional theory calculations of solids *Science* **351** aad3000

[9] Diethelm K 2012 The limits of reproducibility in numerical simulation *Comput. Sci. Eng.* **14** 64–72

[10] Nosek B A and Errington T M 2020 What is replication? *PLoS Biol.* **18** e3000691

[11] Thompson K 1984 Reflections on trusting trust *Commun. ACM* **27** 761–3

[12] Reproducible Builds project 2019 *Reproducible Builds* https://reproducible-builds.org/

[13] ReScience editors 2015 *ReScience C* https://rescience.github.io/

[14] Rougier N P *et al* 2017 Sustainable computational science: the ReScience initiative *PeerJ Comput. Sci.* **3** e142

Computation in Science (Second Edition)
From concepts to practice
Konrad Hinsen

Chapter 7

Outlook: scientific knowledge in the digital age

The goal of scientific research is to discover new scientific knowledge, providing us with a better understanding of the world around us. In this final chapter, I will look at how computation and computing are changing the relation between scientists and scientific knowledge. The impact of these changes has become visible only recently, as it has taken several decades for computing to influence these very foundations of science. It is important for scientists to understand these changes, in order to take advantage of the opportunities they present and to take corrective action wherever they threaten to undermine the reliability and credibility of science.

For centuries, the nature of scientific knowledge had changed very little. It resided first and foremost in the heads of practicing scientists, in the form of factual, procedural, and conceptual knowledge. Factual knowledge consists of the kind of information you could store in tables or diagrams: the density of water, the names of the bones in the human body, the resolution of an instrument, etc. Procedural knowledge is about doing things. At the level of an individual, this can be using a microscope or finding the integral of a function. Examples at the collective level are developing a vaccine, or constructing a synchrotron. Conceptual knowledge consists of principles, classifications, theories, and other means that humans use to organize and reason about facts and actions. Conceptual knowledge relies on abstractions, as I explained in section 5.3, and its acquisition is an important part of what we call understanding.

Since the human brain has a limited capacity for remembering facts reliably, factual knowledge was the first to be recorded. Scientists have always stored detailed factual knowledge in lab notebooks and in reference works. Procedural knowledge soon followed, for example in the form of experimental protocols. Conceptual knowledge is different because we do not tend to forget concepts once we have firmly understood them. Conceptual knowledge is recorded in writing not so much as a memory aid, but for transmitting it to others, in the form of monographs, textbooks, and encyclopedias. A specific form of scientific document, the journal article, was developed for the communication of new discoveries, and usually combines all three forms of knowledge. All scientific knowledge stored in writing is called collectively the *scientific record*.

It is important to understand that the scientific record is a complement to but not a replacement for the knowledge in the heads of scientists, for two reasons. First, the scientific record preserves a trace of contributions and a database of established facts, but says little about the current state of our scientific understanding of the world. If you want to know current scientific consensus on a topic like climate change, you cannot just look it up in a library. You have to ask experts who have followed research on this topic for many years. Second, the contents of the scientific record are largely unintelligible to an untrained person. Interpreting recorded factual knowledge requires very specific conceptual knowledge. A table listing the density of water at different temperatures makes no sense to a person who does not understand the concept of a density, or the definition of temperature. Recorded scientific knowledge builds on more fundamental knowledge that the reader must already possess. General school education provides only a small part of it. All of today's scientists have received personal training from more experienced scientists to prepare them for consulting the scientific record and contributing to it.

Information technologies are currently revolutionizing all aspects of working with scientific knowledge, from its development via its distribution and preservation to its exploitation. In the following, I will briefly discuss the contribution that computation makes to this revolution, leaving aside the at least equally important changes in communication technology, which are profoundly changing how scientists collaborate in making new discoveries.

7.1 The scientific record goes digital

The introduction of computers and computer-controlled machines has changed the storage and retrieval of scientific knowledge in many ways. The most visible change is the transition from printed paper to digital files as the main medium. Books and printed journals are increasingly replaced by databases and Web sites. This has led to profound changes in the economics of scientific publishing. Both the cost of distribution and the cost of access to scientific knowledge have dropped dramatically, and the traditional roles of both publishers and libraries are losing importance. Digital data needs to be curated and preserved as well, but the corresponding roles remain to be defined. A major political struggle is currently going on between the well-established institutions, publishers and research organizations, while at the same time many scientists are experimenting with new technology for scientific communication. Judging from past revolutions in information technology, such as the invention of printing, we can hope to have a better infrastructure for managing scientific knowledge in the end, but in the meantime we will suffer accidental losses, such a Web sites disappearing and hyperlinks rotting.

Information collections that evolve over time mainly fall into one of two categories, which can be described by the metaphors of *streams* and *gardens* [1]. A stream is a timeline of contributions. Traditional examples are bank ledgers and scientific journals, more recent forms are blogs and Twitter timelines. A garden is a resource that is continuously curated to remain up to date. Encyclopedias, both traditional paper editions and modern-day Wikipedia, are the best known examples. In the age of printed paper, gardens were expensive to maintain, and therefore there were only very few of them. In contrast, digital gardens in the form of a Wiki, a database, or an evolving piece of software can be maintained with cheap computing infrastructure, the main cost now being the work of the curators. Unfortunately, the social norms in academia have not yet adapted to this new economic situation. Scientists are judged by their contributions to streams, mainly in the form of journal articles, whereas participation in the curation of gardens is insufficiently appreciated. As a consequence, science is not yet profiting from digital gardens as much as it could.

A major advantage of digital data compared to printed paper is the possibility of automated processing at large scale. Data intensive fields such as bioinformatics could not even have existed before the transition to digital data. Data mining techniques have become commonplace in all domains of research, starting with everyday activities such as the use of Web search engines by scientists. The possibility to tie together information from many different sources is of course highly valuable for science, but it also puts a higher responsibility on each scientist for exercising critical judgment. Unreliable data and the occasional intentional misinformation are the most obvious issues. However, what might turn out to be the most serious problem is information stripped of its context by partially or fully automated processes. Re-using published datasets looks like an obvious gain in productivity, but transplanting them from their original scientific context to another one implies the risk of subtle mistakes, which in turn can undermine the public credibility of science.

7.2 Procedural knowledge turns into software

An important aspect of the digital revolution in science is that procedural knowledge —algorithms—can now be applied without human intervention. Before computers, every action, whether in computation or in doing experiments, was performed by a human. As I pointed out in section 5.3, following a complex sequence of steps requires abstractions, i.e. conceptual knowledge, and thus a minimum of under-standing. Using machines, we can apply stored procedural knowledge without understanding it—in fact, we do this many times every day. We know roughly *what* our machines do, at the highest level of abstraction, but we usually do not understand *how* they do it, nor are we aware of many details that might well be relevant for a specific application. The only way to acquire a deep understanding of how computational models and methods work is to write computer programs that implement them—see section 1.2. Mere users of black-box tools written by others put themselves at risk of making serious mistakes. Statistical irreproducibility (see section 6.3) is one of the symptoms of this development.

The state of today's computing technology wraps digital scientific knowledge in another layer of opacity that could be avoided. In section 4.2.1, I explained the trade-off between performance and clarity in today's programming languages. Formulating algorithms in a way that humans can easily understand and work with requires languages that are more clarity-oriented than anything we have today. In fact, such languages should probably not be called 'programming' languages because their primary purpose would be the communication and preservation of procedural knowledge, rather than its application by a computer. On the other hand, many of today's large-scale simulations are feasible only due to efficient programs that are written in performance-oriented languages. As a consequence of this mismatch, much procedural knowledge of modern science exists only in the form of software that is efficient but unintelligible to its users. It even happens that software becomes unintelligible to its authors over the years, as incidental complexity accumulates (see section 5.5), although few authors will admit this openly. For the first time in the history of science, we have scientific knowledge that we can apply but which no scientist understands any more. A possible antidote could be a wider adoption of the principle of re-editable software (see section 6.7).

The use of programming languages as the only practical notation for scientific algorithms has been particular detrimental to computational models [2]. Models are primarily factual knowledge, stating that certain symbolic representations (equations, graphs, algorithms, etc) mimic the behavior of physical systems at some level of accuracy. What is commonly called a computational model is a model in which the symbolic representation takes the form of an algorithm. Computational scientists tend to focus on tools rather than on models, and thus on software implementing the computational aspect of a model, to the point of believing that the software *is* the model. The factual statements *about* these algorithms and their implementation, which give scientific meaning to the model, are easily neglected. Moreover, in a piece of software, the algorithms representing computational models melt together with other algorithms, such as data munging, user interfaces, or resource management, which often represent the major part of the code of any piece of scientific software. It thus becomes difficult to precisely identify a model. As a consequence, it also becomes very difficult to analyze a model or to compare competing models, even though this ought to be the focus of scientific work. Finally, computational models expressed as software can easily become victims of the complexification described in chapter 5, or get lost as a consequence of software collapse as discussed in section 6.7.

Plain factual data have also been infected by the opacity of scientific software. As I have explained in section 5.3.2, data have their its own abstractions which should be implemented as well-documented data formats based on well-designed data models. In reality, much scientific data are stored using undocumented file formats that are basically some program's internal data structures dumped to a file. The data can thus be used only using a particular program, making it as fragile as the program itself.

7.3 Machine learning: the fusion of factual and procedural knowledge

For a scientist of the pre-computer age, the distinction between factual and procedural knowledge was rather obvious, because the latter was associated with personal action. With the automated application of procedural knowledge by computers, the distinction becomes almost a technical detail. Consider a mathematical function such as the square root. There are well-known algorithms to compute it, but you can also make a table of the results and store it for later lookup[1]. The two approaches differ in the use of resources, but both give the desired result. As a user of mathematical software, you probably don't care how the results are obtained. However, if you want to understand the concept of a square root, the two representations provide very different and complementary perspectives. The table, or better yet a plot of its contents, shows in a direct way how the square root function behaves, whereas the algorithm illustrates its relation to other mathematical concepts.

Machine learning techniques introduce a third way of representing such input-to-output mappings. As I have explained in section 2.2.2, machine learning is based on very generic mathematical models with a large number of parameters that are fitted to a large training dataset. Once trained, a machine learning model is used exactly like an algorithm or a lookup table: they provide output when supplied suitable input. Another way to look at machine learning is as a method for partially converting factual knowledge into procedural knowledge, in much the same way as data compression techniques do.

The use of machine learning techniques in the acquisition and processing of scientific knowledge is very recent and so far best characterized as experimental. Its most optimistic proponents have already announced the end of the scientific method [3] because they believe that machine learning methods will extract from raw data everything one could possibly want to know about the world. At the other end of the spectrum, traditionally minded scientists consider machine learning as no more than sophisticated curve fitting. Both these extreme views will likely turn out to be wrong. The place that machine learning will occupy in the science of the 21st century depends on how useful its peculiar input-to-output mappings will be in reasoning about scientific questions. Current research on machine learning includes the interpretation of the parameters obtained by training, which would obviously be of interest in scientific applications. However, the mere fact that a given input-to-output mapping can be well represented by, say, a neural network of a specific architecture provides information about the system that is described by the mapping, and could possibly be exploited. In the long run, we can expect to see machine learning techniques developed specifically to create interpretable representations, in contrast to today's methods that focus on creating computational tools.

---

[1] I have discussed this partial equivalence between an algorithm and its result in section 2.2.4 as a way to measure the complexity of scientific models.

7.4 The time scales of scientific progress and computing

All knowledge has a finite lifetime. Even if information storage media could be preserved forever, the meaning of the information they contain is ultimately lost because the semantic context in which it was encoded cannot be recorded completely. Extreme examples are historical written documents that nobody can read today, because the languages and writing systems used at the time have been forgotten. Scientific knowledge is particularly vulnerable to becoming lost, because of the large amount of prior knowledge required to make sense of the scientific record.

Written human languages are the most stable semantic contexts we have: they change on a time scale of centuries to millennia. Scientific jargon and scientific notations are more short-lived. Journal articles written 100 years ago are already difficult to understand for today's scientists. The original writings of Galileo or Newton can be read only by scholars specialized in the history of science. The time scale on which original publications remain understandable is a few decades. This does not mean that knowledge is lost that rapidly. As the original writings become less and less clear, the aspects that are recognized as particularly important are constantly reformulated in review articles, monographs, and textbooks. This is why the insights of Galileo and Newton are still accessible to today's physicists.

The advent of computers has not changed the speed of scientific progress on a specific problem. Computers allow us to study more complex phenomena, and attack more questions in parallel, but the translation of individual scientific findings into robust insights relies on humans and still happens on the time scale of years to decades. However, computing technology evolves at a much faster pace. This creates a dilemma for scientific software: as part of the digital garden of scientific knowledge, it should advance at the pace of science, but as a computational tool, it must evolve at the pace of computing technology, as otherwise it becomes unusable (see section 6.7). This evolution is referred to as 'maintenance', a badly chosen metaphor because it suggests that software is subject to wear or decay. It is almost inevitable during maintenance to also change the scientific knowledge embedded in the code, intentionally or by accident. This is one reason why reproducibility, the subject of chapter 6, has become such an important subject in recent years.

The consequence of the different time scales on which scientific knowledge and computing technology evolve is that we are losing access to the original forms of digital scientific knowledge faster than it can be integrated into the reformulation process of science. For many computational studies performed during the last decades, it is already impossible to find the exact models and methods that were used. We are also losing data stored in formats that are defined by software that reads and writes them, if that software is not adequately maintained. To solve this problem, we will have to be more careful about how we store digital scientific knowledge, and in particular make an effort to isolate it from the rapid changes in computing technologies. This requires in particular defining data models and data formats that are independent of specific software packages, and use them to store scientific knowledge in curated digital archives. In some disciplines, in particular the life sciences, this process has already been going on for a few decades.

7.5 The industrialization of science

Taking another step back in looking at the changes to scientific research that computation has already introduced or will likely introduce in the near future, they bear a strong resemblance to the transformations that the industrial revolution has caused in the ways we interact with the material world. In fact, computation provides the same kind of automation for information processing that industrialization enabled for processing matter. We can also observe first structural changes in scientific research that are similar to what happened in the early industrial age.

Since the beginnings of science, researchers have been working like craftspeople. Individuals define personal research projects and execute them using skills and competences they have acquired in a prior phase of apprenticeship to more experienced scientists. Bigger projects are realized through the collaboration of several individuals with different but overlapping skill sets. The findings resulting from a research project are considered personal achievements of their authors and associated with their names. The organizational structures of academia reflect this analogy very well: PhD students are apprentices, postdocs are journeymen, and tenured researchers are masters. Universities take the role of the medieval guilds, overseeing the practice of the crafts but not interfering with the day-to-day work of practitioners as long as it conforms to the established social norms.

Early industrial products were similar to the products of craftspeople they replaced, but due to automation they were cheaper and of more consistent, though not necessarily higher, quality. This is the stage that experimental scientific research has entered with high-throughput techniques, for example in sequencing genomes. The data analysis pipelines that bioinformaticians use to make sense of the resulting genome data can then be seen as the first-stage industrialization of theoretical science. The intellectual credit for the results of these automated procedures is attributed to the people who design the automation process, rather than to those who keep the machines running.

Increased productivity through automation was only the starting point of industrialization. What followed can be described as the emergence of increasingly complex organizational structures for the creation of increasingly complex artifacts, as for example computers. Collaborating craftspeople could never have produced such artifacts, because they lack the structure required to coordinate the large number of specialized experts involved in sophisticated technologies. Today's hierarchically organized companies coordinate the efforts of hundreds to thousands of people. But production is only one aspect of complex artifacts. They also need to be evaluated, sold, and maintained, and their impact on public goods such as the environment or public health requires regulation by public authorities. Industrial products are thus characterized by the many roles that people take in relation to them, with each role requiring specific competences. Designing and producing computers, developing software, and using computers plus software are examples of such distinct roles and competences.

The transformation of scientific methods into black-box tools that I have outlined in section 7.2 can thus be seen as the second stage of the industrialization of scientific research. The roles of software developers and software users become distinct, following the lead of commodity software outside of science. The keyword that signals this stage of industrialization is 'reusable', implying the creation of products meant to be used by someone else than the original author. It is also increasingly applied to scientific datasets, as part of the FAIR (findable, accessible, interoperable, reusable) principles [4]. Datasets are thus also on the way to becoming industrial products.

Many of the problematic aspects of computation in science that I have mentioned in this book are symptoms of an incomplete transition to an industrial style of working. In the world of craftspeople, individual scientists are expected to understand the context in which data were collected and the analysis methods they apply to them. In a world of reusable but also more complex datasets and software-based methods, this is no longer possible, leading to symptoms such as statistical irreproducibility (see section 6.3). Likewise, craftspeople doing computational science have an intimate knowledge of their software tools, which are designed to be re-editable rather than reusable (see section 6.7). With complex reusable software, they cannot retain full mastery of their software installations, and suffer computational irreproducibility (see section 6.4).

There are of course important differences between the production of material goods and the creation of immaterial goods. For example, economies of scale play a major role in the former, but are absent in the latter. There is an even more important particularity in scientific research, whose goal is discovery. Discovery cannot be planned and thus cannot be organized on a large scale. For the foreseeable future, research is likely to be dominated by the work of craftspeople, with industry-like 'Big Science' remaining a complement. However, these craftspeople will use industrially produced tools (software) and components (datasets) for their work, much like a modern-day carpenter does. What remains to be worked out is the interfaces between industrial producers and the craftspeople working with their outputs.

One important aspect of these interfaces is where they are situated in knowledge space. An industrial product makes sense only if its users can operate with a much more limited knowledge of its characteristics than its producers. Industrial products must be specifically designed to be safe to use under such conditions. For example, a car whose driver can only drive safely if he or she is aware of the inner workings of the braking system is not acceptable. What this means for the designer is that the product's user interface must be composed of robust abstractions (see section 5.3). This is not the case today for most scientific software, and even less for published datasets. Safe use of these supposedly reusable items requires collaboration with their authors or with a community of power users.

The social aspects of defining the interfaces between industrial products and craftspeople also require further attention. We need auxiliary professions and institutions that formulate best practices for the development, documentation, and use of industrially produced tools in science, and oversee their correct application. We must develop the analogues of user manuals, quality labels, expert evaluations, certified training, and safety regulations that have evolved at the interface of craft and industry elsewhere. Reproducibility, the subject of chapter 6, is already becoming a quality label, and certification agencies such as CASCaD [5] or CODECHECK [6] have started to offer expert services for attributing this label. Data management plans are an early example of regulation. As with quality labels and regulations in traditional industries, they do not promise perfection. Reproducible results can be wrong, and data managed according to best practices can contain mistakes. The goal is not unattainable perfection, but establishing trust in the work of others that one cannot verify oneself.

7.6 Preparing the future

In the early days of computing, in the 1950s and 1960s, technology was driven by the needs of scientific users, who were the most demanding clients at the time. In the following decades, computers have found their way into all aspects of our lives and the only computing technology that is still dominated by scientific applications is high-performance computing. In spite of the latter's high visibility, it represents a small fraction of the computing technology that scientists use for their daily work. With the exception of domain-specific scientific software, all of the technology that scientists use was developed outside of the scientific community and often for very different applications. As a consequence, scientists have started to consider computing technology as imposed from the outside. Few of today's computational scientists would even consider working with computer scientists or computer manufacturers on technological developments that better fit their needs.

All the problematic aspects that I have mentioned in this chapter can be traced back to the lack of technological developments that cover the specific requirements of scientific computing. Computer scientists do not develop better formal languages for scientific models because nobody asks for them. Programming languages are not tailor-made for scientific computing, except for high-performance languages, because scientists do not clearly state their needs. Reproducibility and long-term stability are not priorities in the design of computing systems, because scientists do not even envisage requesting them.

Computers have become so important for scientific research that computational scientists should care about their development with the same enthusiasm that their experimental colleagues show for the improvement of lab instruments. In other words, scientists must take a more active part in the development of computing technology again, at all levels from hardware via systems software and applications software to the management of scientific data. I hope that this book will contribute to this process by giving its readers sufficient background knowledge that they can formulate their requirements and discuss them with computer scientists, software engineers, and hardware designers. Ultimately, this will benefit everyone by leading to better science.

7.7 Further reading

The transformation of the concept of knowledge in the context of the information explosion caused by computers and the Internet is the subject of David Weinberger's *Too Big to Know* [7]. Ann Blair's similarly titled *Too much to know* [8] discusses the same problem in the historical context of the invention of the printing press.

The new communication technologies that were made possible by computers and the Internet are also likely to introduce profound changes into the process of doing scientific research. This topic is explored in detail by Michael Nielsen's *Reinventing Discovery* [9]. Another good use for new technologies is better explanation of scientific concepts and findings. The Web site 'Explorable Explanations' provides many examples, to which Bret Victor's 'Media for Thinking the Unthinkable' adds theoretical underpinnings.

An impressive example of publicly shared datasets explained through tutorials with embedded code is provided by the tutorials of the LIGO project on the observation of gravitational waves.

The use of computers for the generation or verification of mathematical proofs is the subject of an ongoing debate [10–12] about the status of computer-generated knowledge. A famous example is the proof of the four-color theorem [13].

My own contribution to improving the management of scientific knowledge in the context of computation is the development of a Digital Scientific Notation for physics and chemistry [14, 15] which is intended to permit the definition of computational models in journal articles and textbooks rather than exclusively in software.

References

[1] Caulfield M 2015 The garden and the stream: a technopastoral https://hapgood.us/2015/10/17/the-garden-and-the-stream-a-technopastoral/
[2] Hinsen K 2014 Computational science: shifting the focus from tools to models [v2; ref status: indexed, http://f1000r.es/3p2] *F1000Research* **3** 101
[3] Anderson C 2008 The end of theory: the data deluge makes the scientific method obsolete *Wired*
[4] GO FAIR Initiative 2019 *FAIR Principles* https://web.archive.org/web/20191202184853/https://www.go-fair.org/fair-principles/.
[5] CASCaD - Certification Agency for Scientific Code & Data 2019 https://www.cascad.tech/.
[6] Eglen S and Nüst D 2020 *CODECHECK* https://codecheck.org.uk/.
[7] Weinberger D 2011 *Too Big to Know: Rethinking Knowledge Now that the Facts Aren't the Facts, Experts are Everywhere, and the Smartest Person in the Room is the Room* (New York: Basic Books)
[8] Blair A 2010 *Too Much to Know: Managing Scholarly Information before the Modern Age* (New Haven, CT: Yale University Press)
[9] Nielsen M 2013 *Reinventing Discovery: The New Era of Networked Science* reprint edn (Princeton, NJ: Princeton University Press)
[10] Thurston W P 1994 *On proof and Progress in Mathematics* (arXiv:math/9404236)

[11] Wolchover N 2013 In computers we trust? *Simons Foundation* https://simonsfoundation.org/features/science-news/in-computers-we-trust.

[12] Hartnett K 2015 *Univalent Foundations Redefines Mathematics* https://www.quantamagazine.org/univalent-foundations-redefines-mathematics-20150519/.

[13] Gonthier G 2008 Formal proof—the four-color theorem *Not. Am. Math. Soc.* 55 1382–93

[14] Hinsen K 2016 *Scientific Notations for the Digital Era* (arXiv:1605.02960 [physics])

[15] Hinsen K 2018 Verifiability in computer-aided research: The role of digital scientific notations at the human-computer interface *PeerJ Comput. Sci.* **4** e158

Lightning Source UK Ltd.
Milton Keynes UK
UKHW051315091220
374844UK00002B/35